HIDDEN
VILLAGES
OF BRITAIN

HIDDEN VILLAGES OF BRITAIN

HISTORIES AND TRADITION PAST AND PRESENT

BATSFORD

First published in the United Kingdom in 2017 by B.T. Batsford
43 Great Ormond Street
London WC1N 3HZ

An imprint of B.T. Batsford Holdings Ltd

ISBN: 9781849944489

A CIP catalogue record for this book is available from the British Library.

10 9 8 7 6 5

Reproduction by Colour Depth, UK
Printed by Toppan Leefung Printing Ltd, China

This book can be ordered direct from the publisher at the website:
www.batsfordbooks.com or try your local bookshop.

With thanks to Reef Television and More4.

Page 2: A Brian Cook artwork used as a poster for the British Travel and Holidays Association.

Page 5: A scene of the Sussex Weald by Brian Cook, used for the cover of *South Eastern Survey* by Richard Wyndham, 1940.

CONTENTS

BRIAN COOK — '40

Introduction

There are more than 10,000 villages in Britain, each with its own tale to tell of historical shenanigans, hard graft and contemporary larks. From woodland settlements, to coastal fishing villages, from mining communities in Wales and Cornwall, to northern villages forged by industry, they are all places of work, traditions and community. What they are not is places mired in the past: four million British people live in villages and they continue to flourish and develop with initiatives like farmers' markets and community-run shops and pubs breathing new life into centuries-old settlements.

A brief history of villages

The story of Britain's villages is as old as its people. Prehistoric man gathered together in wooden hut circles and, come the Iron Age, hamlets sprang up to house the farming populace. The Romans imposed order on unruly communities, with straight roads and villages laid out on rectilinear grids, but this was only a blip: once they had gone, the settlements returned to haphazard agricultural hamlets.

Order was restored once again with the Anglo Saxons in the late 600s, and villages spread across central England, replacing scattered homesteads. A new grid system of horizontal and vertical axes was introduced, as were boundaries, enclosures and regular plots. Barns and mills also appeared in many of the wealthier communities.

But it was after the Norman invasion of 1066 that the village as we recognise it was born. Cottages were built along streets around a central focus, usually a church, bridge, mill or manor house presided over by the lord of the manor. The poorer folk lived in wattle and daub cottages, which, if they were lucky, had their own private courtyard, vegetable patch and pen to keep an animal or two. The size of the village depended on whether it had a market. If it did, it was held in the nave of the church on Sundays, until protests from the clergy forced them out into the street or marketplace, which became the village's new hub. Often, these larger villages grew to become market towns with a charter to hold markets or fairs.

Many of these elements still exist in contemporary villages, augmented by more recent additions, such as a pub, shop, village hall or post office. Although

cottages from before 1600 are unlikely to have survived, newer homes are often built on their footprint, so the layout of a village often remains the same. As the centuries have rolled on, each village has evolved and grown on a piecemeal basis. Different styles of vernacular architecture, from timber-framed cottages to Victorian brick buildings, sit, side by side, embodying a 3D-representation of the village's history.

The history of each British village is colourful and action-packed – don't be fooled by its tranquil and often idyllic appearance: an intriguing and hidden world lies beneath the thatched roofs and church bell towers waiting to be discovered.

What is a village?

Although there is no strict definition, a village is generally defined as a small settlement in a rural setting. It is larger than a hamlet (which earns the right to call itself a village when a church is built), and smaller than a town. Most have agricultural, quarrying, fishing or mining origins: homes were built where the work was. The population of villages ranges from a few hundred to a few thousand, and most are clustered around a central point, most frequently a church or village green – known as a nucleated settlement – although some are strung along a river or line a clifftop. Villages are considered idyllic places to live, far from the noise and pace of city life, and with a close and supportive population.

This is not the full picture, of course: many have become dormitory places for commuters, with many facilities such as pubs and village stores disappearing. As bus routes vanish, villages can be claustrophobic and isolating places to inhabit for those without cars. A new spirit is afoot however, with committed and active villagers taking control of pubs and stores, ensuring that ancient traditions and customs are kept alive and holding annual village events that bring life into the village's heart.

Left: Alfriston Clergy House in East Sussex.
Above: A rural idyll shown in a Batsford guide.

The artist behind the Batsford guides

During the 1930s, a small publishing house, Batsford, produced a series of books that captured the essence of British rural life. The subjects covered included villages, gardens, castles, cottages, county guides, and elements of the landscape, including hills, seashore and trees. They were a snapshot of British country life, chronicling the world of work – haymaking and ploughing, fishermen at their nets – as well as villages clustered around the church or village green, and the rolling and verdant landscape that surrounded them.

While the authors varied from one title to another, one man was responsible for their memorable covers. Brian Cook Batsford's instantly recognisable artwork with its carefully drawn images and large areas of flat, bright colour, sang out from the bookshelves. His distinctive style, with its bold use of clashing colours, boosted sales of the books, which are still keenly collected today. The consistency of the covers was largely because Brian Cook worked as an illustrator and designer at Batsford for 20 years, from 1928 until 1950. After studying at Repton Art School, he went to work for his publisher uncle Harry Batsford, even changing his name to Brian Batsford at Harry's request in 1946 – Harry had no heirs and Brian was to inherit the company.

Below (left to right): *The Legacy of England*, published in 1935; *How to See the Country*, part of the series of *Home Front* handbooks published in 1940.

The financial crisis of 1929–31, prompted Harry Batsford to dispense with the services of authors and illustrators and most writers. The only survivors of this staff cull were Charles Fry (who wrote the guides with Harry) and Brian. The first book cover designed by Brian was *The Villages of England* when he was 21, followed by *The Landscape of England*, whose jacket was the village of Combe Martin, featured on page 170 of this book.

Brian pioneered the use of the Jean Berté watercolour printing process, in which plates were cut in soft rubber and printed with water-based inks, rather than oil. A separate plate was used for each colour, which accounts for the blocks of colour in Brian's work. Brian had little regard for the finished product and threw away the covers or 'wrappers' as he called them, placing books on his shelves in their cloth bindings. Fortunately, the production manager at Batsford, Francis Lucarotti, kept every jacket safe in an album.

Brian Cook Batsford inherited the business when Uncle Harry died in 1952. Unfortunately for lovers of his artwork, his new responsibilities as Chairman (a position he held until 1974) meant that his output as an illustrator and designer dwindled. He threw his energy into running the company and into his duties as Conservative MP for Ealing South. Despite the change in his circumstances, his love for the British countryside endured. He moved frequently, living all over Britain, all the while taking an active interest in the conservation of buildings and the countryside. After retiring, Brian returned to painting, and when he was 75, he exhibited new work at the Hayward Gallery and the Parkin Gallery. He died in the appropriately scenic village of Winchelsea in 1991.

ARGYLL AND BUTE

Sitting between Glasgow, Loch Lomond and the Western Isles, Argyll and Bute is an area that often gets overlooked. This is a shame as its villages – sprinkled around the ragged coastline, overlooking deep sea lochs and scattered across the islands of the Inner Hebrides – are well worth seeking out.

This is a landscape of peninsulas and islands where boats are as essential as cars for getting about. More ferry journeys are made in this region than any other part of Scotland, taking locals and visitors to and fro over the sea lochs between fingers of land, including the famous Mull of Kintyre.

The Batsford guide to the region described the area's villages as 'usually consisting of little more than a single street of low, whitewashed houses following the main road or fronting a loch. With a general shop, a school and one or more small kirks.' Things have moved on since then, of course, and although the villages are still remote, many have adapted to change and are now thriving communities.

Tarbert: A bridge between two lochs

During the early 1900s, you could cross the harbour at Tarbert by walking from one fishing boat to the other. The village was shaped by herring fishing, with 88 boats setting sail daily across Loch Fyne, each with a four-man crew. Evidence of herrings were everywhere – shopkeepers would find fish scales in their tills, deposited from the coins of fishermen.

Times change, of course, and although the fishing boats no longer go out, Tarbert is still a bustling and lively village and home to 1,000 residents. Its position on an isthmus little more than 1 mile (1.6km) wide at the narrowest point of the Kintyre peninsula, means that life in Tarbert will always be about the sea and about boats. Every July, the village's Traditional Boat Festival attracts vessels and visitors from all over the UK for a weekend of activities that nod to Tarbert's maritime past.

Another important element of the village's past is the legend of Magnus Barefoot, a young King of Norway who repeatedly raided the west coast of Scotland on longships in 1093. Under constant siege, King Malcolm of Scotland thought it was time to broker a deal with the Viking. He said that Magnus could have all the islands off the west coast separated by water and navigable by ship. When Magnus reached Kintyre he sat at the helm of his boat as the crew hauled it over the isthmus at Tarbert, thus deviously turning it into an island to plunder at will. This legend is re-enacted by villagers every year when they drag a longship from the far loch through the village to the harbour.

Crinan: All about connections

For 200 years, the village of Crinan with its lighthouse, hotel and café, has been a canal service station, albeit a very pretty one. Situated on the western end of the Crinan Canal, it has seen cargo boats, fishing vessels and more recently yachts, sail past and out into the Sound of Jura. The canal is a man-made waterway connecting Glasgow with the Western Isles thus avoiding the need to sail around the often-treacherous Mull of Kintyre. Nine miles (14.5km) long,

Above: The village economy at Tarbert was reliant upon herring fishing.
Left: The harbour at Tarbert, seen across Loch Fyne.

it links Loch Fyne to the Atlantic, and rises from sea level to 65ft (19.8m) and back down again, passing through 15 locks and under seven swing bridges. Its construction in 1801 meant that working vessels could make the journey to the ocean with speed and in safety.

Crinan was really put on the map, however, during a royal visit in 1847. Queen Victoria, Albert and the children were touring the west coast when they realised that the canal was a handy short cut. They boarded a decorated horse-drawn barge and set off accompanied by cheering crowds.

Following their lead, 40,000 people took a similar journey, bringing prosperity and change to the villages along the canal's route. Steamers ran trips from Loch Fyne to the canal's entrance at Ardrishaig, where passengers disembarked to board a canal boat, *The Linnet*. Trips up and down the canal were tremendously popular and went at a leisurely pace so tourists had plenty of time to take in the sights and spend their money as they went. Nowadays, it's mostly yachts that sail out of Crinan heading out to sea and the Western Islands beyond.

Kerrycroy village: Built with love

Argyll and Bute has the most inhabited islands of any part of Scotland. The Isle of Bute is one of them and is the location of a charming and unexpected village: Kerrycroy. Seven half-timbered, Tudor-style buildings sit overlooking a sea loch and a village green. The story of how this very un-Scottish settlement came to be built is all about the house in whose grounds it was built: Mount Stuart.

This extravagant neo-Gothic building is the seat of the Marquess of Bute. The family still owns most of the island but in the 19th century their wealth and power was legendary, extending as far as South Wales, where they were involved with the docks and the coal trade.

This wealth is manifest in Mount Stuart, which is said to contain more Italian marble than any other house in Britain. It was also the first home in Scotland to be lit by electricity, centrally heated and with its own telephone system. It was also the first anywhere to boast a heated indoor pool, Roman innovations aside.

Kerrycroy was the project of the 2nd Marquess of Bute and his first wife, Maria North, who wanted her own private village away from the house. The Marquess had made his fortune as an industrialist (he built Cardiff Docks) but led a relatively secluded life at Mount Stuart. In 1818, to please the

THE THRILL OF THE FERRY

Watching your destination appear on the horizon from the top deck of a ferry is one of the most romantic ways to travel. Feeling the sea spray as the hull of the boat breaks the waves and watching seabirds dive for fish is a refreshing change from being cooped up in a car.

Part of the pleasure of visiting the Western islands of Scotland is getting there on the ferry. Successful trips depend on a thorough knowledge of the Caledonina MacBrayne ferry timetable. The company, known as Calmac, is the main ferry company connecting the mainland with its peninsulas and with the islands of the Inner and Outer Hebrides. These routes are classified as 'lifeline services' and are vital to the inhabitants of the islands who rely on them for essentials and to get to and from the mainland.

Not all Scottish ferries are Calmac, though. The ferry to Easdale, which takes children to their schools in Oban and brings provisions back is run by four local ferrymen who live on the island with their families and there are similar small operations all over the country.

FIVE BRITISH FERRY JOURNEYS TO VILLAGES

1. Mull to Iona, Scotland
Leave the car at Fionnphort on Mull and hop on the ferry to Iona. Ten minutes later you will alight on the white sandy beaches of Scotland's most spiritual island.

2. Falmouth to St Mawes, Cornwall
A mind-clearing trip from bustling Falmouth across the wide-open mouth of the Carrick Roads estuary to the delightful village of St Mawes with its fish restaurants and attractive seafront.

3. Sandbanks to Studland, Dorset
A quick jaunt across Poole Harbour takes you from the opulence of Sandbanks and its millionaire's homes to the dunes and villages of Purbeck including Corfe Castle.

4. Southwold to Walberswick, Suffolk
A row boat transports foot passengers from the seaside town of Southwold to the tea rooms, pubs and galleries of Walberswick.

5. Portsmouth to Fishbourne, Isle of Wight
Leave the busy harbour of Portsmouth behind and begin exploration of The Isle of Wight at this village beside a creek.

Marchioness, who was a little homesick for England, her husband agreed that she could design a model village in the grounds in a quasi-English style. The village has half-timbered houses, a village pub and a school. It was inhabited by workers from the estate but was created as a gift.

Gigha: A real island community

Gigha looks like a traditional island with a grocer, a post office and a hardware shop, but unlike neighbouring islands, it is run in a most unusual way. The tiny island – 7 miles (11.3km) long and 1½ miles (2.4km) wide – is currently home to 165 residents. It is a thriving community with well-run amenities, but it has not always been like this.

Over a period of many years, a succession of landowning lairds bought and sold the island for profit, neglecting its infrastructure and not investing in its future. When Gigha was put up for sale once again in 2001, the islanders decided to take matters into their own hands. At the time, there were 87 residents on Gigha, many of who were retired and from fishing and farming backgrounds. Nevertheless, the islanders, encouraged by their local MP, established the Gigha Heritage Trust and raised the £1 million necessary to buy the island; they then went on to raise a further £4 million to improve facilities and infrastructure, from drains to new housing.

One of the Trust's initiatives has been to install wind turbines, known locally as the Dancing Ladies of Gigha. These not only provide sustainable energy but create revenue: surplus power is sold back to the national grid and the income raised has been invested in building snug, warm eco houses.

A short walk from the village takes you to Achamore House and Gardens, once the home of the laird, but now managed by the Trust. The 54-acre (21.8ha) estate with its walled garden and woodland requires a lot of manpower to maintain. True to the spirit of the island, volunteers pitch in to help with a range of tasks from weeding to grass cutting.

Above: Cows on the island of Gigha, with the 'Dancing Ladies' in the background.
Left: The ferry leaves the shore at Gigha.

Tighnabruaich: A shinty village

Stretching along the edge of the Kyles of Bute sea channel, the villas of this pretty town have a distinctly Victorian air, especially when the world's last seagoing paddle steamer, *The Waverley*, sails past on its way to Arran and Bute.

Things are less genteel on the town's sports ground, which also overlooks the loch: this is home to Kyles Athletic, one of the best shinty teams in Scotland. For those unsure of what shinty is, the Batsford guide describes the game brilliantly: 'This lively pastime might be called hockey in the rough, with no nonsense about it. Sticks and rules of a relatively free and easy kind. It's the sort of game that village boys might improvise with crooked bows and a knot of wood on the common land in the evening.'

Shinty arrived in Scotland from Ireland 1,000 years ago. Today there are 3,000 registered players and 38 of the 50 clubs are based in small communities like Tighnabruaich. The village is also the home of the shinty stick, which is made by three generations of the Blair family – Neil, John and Christopher – all shinty players themselves. Unlike cricket and hockey, shinty players use different sticks depending on the position in which they play. Each stick is made from hickory and can take several days to make.

Easdale: A slate island

This tiny island of just 25 acres (10.1ha) was once the unlikely capital of the Scottish slate industry. Roof slate mined in its seven quarries has been used on buildings all over the world, as far away as Australia and Canada. Easdale's quarries were most productive in the 1700s when 500 people lived here. However, in 1850 a storm flooded all the quarries and, with no means of pumping out the water, this put an end to the island's slate economy. The quarries became pools of water and the village shrank to four people; it looked as if Easdale was going to become a forgotten island.

Fortunately a new community sprang up, and there are now 71 homes on the island, as well as a folk museum, a concert hall, a shop and a pub. Much of

Above: A 19th-century engraving depicting a game of shinty.

this is due to the work of the Easdale Island Community Development Group, which is run by residents. The village's heritage can be seen in the slate roofs of the former miners' cottages, which glisten prettily in the rain due to a high percentage of iron pyrite (also known as fool's gold).

Slate is also the driving force behind Easdale's new international notoriety. Every September, the island hosts the World Stone Skimming Championships in one of its disused quarries. This is much more than a village sport: up to 350 stone skimmers travel here from as far as Poland and India to take part. They compete to skim a piece of slate the furthest (it must bounce at least three times) and competition is fierce and lively: an unusual but effective way to keep the island flourishing.

Above: The World Stone Skimming Championships, held annually at Easdale.

Stone skimming and shinty are just two of the sports that are enjoyed in British villages. They may sound unfamiliar but they serve the same purpose as more familiar games like cricket: they bring everyone together, and encourage friendly competition with other communities.

Village cricket, the thwack of a ball as it is sent flying into shrubbery and the ripple of applause that accompanies it, are the quintessential soundtrack to a British summer. Village cricket may appear genteel and well-mannered but it is also seriously competitive. Many villages have their own teams and compete in local and regional club cricket leagues. Some go as far as entering the National Village Cup competition, which is open to villages with populations below 5,000 in England, Scotland and Wales. Every year around 300 clubs take part with the final being played at Lord's Cricket Ground in London.

FIVE CURIOUS VILLAGE GAMES

Bog snorkelling

Competitors complete two lengths of a 55m water-filled trench cut through a peat bog. They must wear snorkels and flippers and complete the course by flipper power alone. The soggy activity takes place in the Waen Rhydd peat bog near Llanwrtyd Wells in Wales. The Current (2016) champion is Daniel Norman who completed the course in 1 min 26.38 seconds.

Dwile flonking

The first game, which was re-created from the memories of the Michael Bentine original, was recorded in 1965 in Leeds. One team forms a circle and dances around as a member of the other team enters the circle and attempts to soak them with a beer-soaked dwile (cloth). The game takes place at a different village pub every year.

Gravy wrestling

This relatively new sport – it began in 2007 as part of a food festival – takes place in Stacksteads in Lancashire. The annual World Gravy Wrestling Championships bouts are fought in a pool filled with some unspecified gloopy brown liquid (not gravy).

Coconut shy

Most often found at village fêtes, this game, which dates back to the late 1800s, consists of throwing wooden balls at rows of coconuts balanced on posts. Any player successfully dislodging a coconut wins either the coconut or a prize. (The word 'shy' means to toss or throw.)

Cheese rolling

Originally intended for the residents of Brockworth village, this scramble down a hill after a 9lb (4kg) round of Double Gloucester now draws competitors from all over the world. It takes place every Spring Bank Holiday at Cooper's Hill near Gloucester, and the first person over the finish line wins the cheese. Many injuries are incurred in the process.

ROYAL DEESIDE

The villages of Royal Deeside in Aberdeenshire lie along the valley of the River Dee, which rises in the Cairngorms and rushes down to the North Sea at Aberdeen. Upstream there are fewer than eight people for every square mile (2.6sq. km), distributed in small settlements scattered across huge estates. The landscape remains unspoiled and unpopulated largely because over 500,000 acres (202,342ha) are predominantly owned by just ten people.

There is no shortage of majesty in this region: rural Aberdeenshire between Braemar and Banchory is not just a region of vast open spaces, mountains and the tumultuous River Dee, but it is the place that Queen Victoria loved so much she built a castle there – Balmoral. Since then, the British royal family have spent their summers at Balmoral and attend the Braemar Gathering and Highland Games every September: no wonder it is called Royal Deeside.

Aboyne, Dinnet and Lochnagar

Aboyne, on the edge of the Highlands, is the largest village on Deeside. Its size owes much to the building of a road adjacent to the river 250 years ago, which made the village accessible for the first time. When the road was joined by a railway, the village became an even more important crossing point on the river. The Batsford guide to Royal Deeside describes the approach to the village: 'The road to Aboyne, after the soft hillside, was hard and unexciting although it passed through a dense wood out of reach of sun and one could stand on the bridge over the Dee enjoying for the first time the sweep and rush of a great river.'

Off the main road the atmosphere and landscape changes as Craigendinnie rises steeply, offering opportunities for gliding and good views of Aboyne below. Unsurprisingly, villages become scarcer the higher you go. The village of Dinnet is one of these, and although small, it is often called the gateway to the Cairngorms National Park and to the Highlands.

Lochnagar is the highest point of the Queen's Balmoral estate. It has a couple of literary associations: the poet Lord Byron lived in the area and wrote a poem about it:

Above: The old military road through the hills, which links Fettercairn and Aboyne.

'England! thy beauties are tame and domestic
To one who has roamed o'er the mountains afar
Oh for the crags that are wild and majestic,
The steep frowning glories o' dark Lochnagar'.

The Prince of Wales also used it as the setting for his children's book, *The Old Man of Lochnagar*, that tells the story of an old man who lives in a cave overlooking Balmoral. A huge fan of Deeside, where he spent many childhood holidays, the Prince has said there is no place on earth like it.

Ballater and the Royals

Let the Batsford guide provide an introduction to this pretty village, which is popular with hikers and Royals alike: 'Ballater is very pleasantly placed where the Dee valley makes a wide sweep between well-wooded hills, one of which is Craigendarroch, that's the one, the special feature of the locality. Groups of villas and cottages cluster around the green, in the centre of which the new Parish church of the Church of Scotland, rears its graceful spire.'

As it's very close to Balmoral (7½ miles/12km to the west), the village of Ballater has more than any other benefited from 160 years of Royal patronage and several shops here are by Royal Appointment. In 1886 it became the terminus of the new railway line from Aberdeen. The intention was to take the line further up the valley but Queen Victoria wasn't taken with the prospect of a railway so close to Balmoral, so that plan was scrapped. Nonetheless, the Royal Family arrived at Ballater station every summer for their annual visit until 1966, when Dr Richard Beeching's report on the state of British railways (see box, page 28) led to the line being axed.

When Queen Victoria and her husband Prince Albert first visited the Highlands they both fell in love with the area. The forested mountains and sparkling rivers reminded Albert of his German homeland, and Victoria saw it as a place that offered privacy and escape. They found their Scottish home in Deeside, an estate of over 50,000 acres (202,342ha) of land, with Balmoral Castle at its heart. Although Victoria described the castle as 'small but pretty' it was deemed too restricting for the growing Royal Family and Albert, working with the architect William Smith, reinvented it in Scots baronial style in 1856.

Above: Balmoral Castle. Since 1852 it has been the private residence of each monarch. The rest of us can have a look around in the spring and summer when its grounds are open to the public.

You can still see evidence of the railway network that once connected many British villages, including Ballater, if you look out for it. Disused straight and flat railway tracks have become walkers' routes or cycle paths, and railway stations have been converted into character homes or cafés. Some lines even still operate on a small scale as heritage railways with steam trains puffing up and down.

Once considered a vital part of rural life, branch lines and their stations fell victim to cuts following two reports made by Dr Richard Beeching. *The Reshaping of British Railways* (1963) and *The Development of the Major Railway Trunk Routes* (1965) were published by the British Railways Board and identified 2,363 stations and 5,000 miles (8,047km) of railway line for closure. This represented 55 per cent of stations and 30 per cent of route miles.

Beeching was clear-eyed and unsentimental about the cuts. His brief was to stem the large losses caused by increased competition from road transport and the reduction in rail subsidies, which he approached as a simple profit-and-loss exercise as British Rail was losing £140m a day.

Yorkshire Dales
BY L·N·E·R
"THE HOLIDAY HANDBOOK"
Over 1,100 pages   Illustrations in Photogravure
Maps   Street Plans   Details of Accommodation
From Booksellers or L·N·E·R Agencies   Price 6d

Some of the lines he put forward for closure had never been profitable and were barely used, and many were in a poor state of repair. Others, however, provided a vital service to local communities who had no other means of public transport. Their loss would result in swathes of the country becoming cut off with a knock-on effect on tourism and other commercial activities. Protests against closures drew considerable support, with petitions and demonstrations championed by poet Sir John Betjeman, but in spite of this most of Beeching's suggested cuts were implemented. Beeching had proposed that a better bus service be provided in place of the railway network but this was never delivered.

More recently, campaigns have sprung up to reverse the cuts and hundreds of miles of track have been slowly reopened and stations refurbished. However, these heritage lines are the result of the work of local enthusiasts and volunteers, and are nowhere near the scale of the original network.

Finzean and the village shop

Deeside's vast stretches of undeveloped estates, incorporating farmland, forestry and moorland, are maintained by just a few communities. One of these is Finzean, a village of just 400 people, who mostly serve the 10,000-acre (4,047ha) Finzean Estate. The land and its wild game, including the herd of deer, is managed by a gamekeeper who, among other things, is responsible for keeping the number of deer in check and delivering the venison produced by any culls to the village shop.

The Finzean Estate Farm Shop is a showcase for local suppliers and, as well as venison and other game, sells produce from the Estate and other local producers, including honey, vegetables, preserves and cheese. It has become a community hub and is a cheering example of the revival of village shops (see page 32) that are beginning to flourish nationally.

Above: Highland stags are among the wildlife found on the Finzean Estate.

The Painting Laird

One of Finzean's former Lairds, Joseph Farquharson, was also a well-loved artist who painted many local scenes, notably snowy landscapes that are still popular as Christmas cards today. He inherited the Finzean Estate in 1918 and spent the rest of his life as part-estate manager and part-respected artist. A trained painter, he spent much time outdoors in a specially constructed painting hut on wheels that allowed him to paint throughout the winter. Many of his paintings depict sheep in snowy scenes (he was jokingly referred to as 'Frozen Mutton Farquharson' by contemporaries), and when there were no sheep handy, he used one or two provided by a local taxidermist as models. The Painting Laird died in 1935, but during his lifetime he had 200 works exhibited at the Royal Academy. His paintings of the landscape and people around Finzean were popular at the time and are still sought-after and valued today.

Tarland and its fiddle-playing tradition

The village of Tarland, 5 miles (8km) from Aboyne, appears to be a sleepy backwater to the unknowing visitor, but don't be fooled: its 500 residents know how to party. Drop into the village pub most evenings and the place comes alive with the sound of the fiddle.

Fiddle playing is as much of a Deeside tradition as bagpipes, cabers and kilts. Tarland has produced world-class players since the mid-19th century when Peter Milne, known as the Tarland Minstrel, gained national popularity. Milne travelled the country extensively to give performances and his compositions are considered among the finest of all Scottish fiddle pieces. He was a professional musician, a dancing master, and led orchestras in Aberdeen, Leith, Edinburgh and Manchester. He also played for Queen Victoria at Balmoral where he received a silver medal for his 'pathetic rendering of "Auld Robin Gray" at Balmoral.'

Tarland man Paul Anderson, a fiddle player, composer and tutor, is continuing the tradition. Similarly inspired by the landscape and the history of the area, he is one of the most respected exponents of fiddle playing performing today.

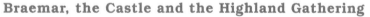

Braemar, the Castle and the Highland Gathering

The history of Braemar is as wild as the surrounding mountains and forests. Deeside's highest village was once part of the territory ruled by the Highland clans, the kinship groups that enforced law and order. Their domination of the Cairngorms ended when their castle, a fully functioning fortress and military base, was burned in 1689 during the Jacobite uprising to restore Scottish Catholic James VII to the throne. It was subsequently bought by John Farquharson and left in ruins until 1748 when it was leased to the Government as a garrison, returning to the Farquharson clan in 1831.

As the years went on, the castle fell into disrepair, and in 2006 the family decided to sell. A group of local people stepped up to save it; they leased it from

Above: Evening sun falls across ploughed fields at Tarland.

the owners, and created a charitable foundation, Braemar Community Ltd, to manage it. Through donations (some from the Prince of Wales who used to play there as a child) and events, they raised enough money to repair the fabric of the building. The castle reopened to the public in 2008, and is manned by 40 local volunteers for seven months a year. There is still a daunting amount of work to do, however, with a further £700,000 required to complete restoration and repairs.

The Braemar Gathering

Smaller games can be found throughout the Highlands, but Braemar is home to the most famous – the Braemar Gathering. Although gatherings of one sort or another have been held at Braemar for 900 years, the Gathering has gained momentum and status since 1832 when the Braemar Royal Highland Society took over its organization. Royalty has also given the event a boost: Queen Victoria was the first monarch to visit and her attendance pushed it to even greater prominence. Queen Elizabeth II has been a fixture throughout her reign, attending every year, when she has the honour of being acclaimed as Chieftain of the Braemar Gathering.

Although the Gathering keeps growing, many of the original competitive events, including throwing the hammer and tossing the caber, remain the same. But there have been new additions over the years, such as Highland dancing, bagpipes, tug of war and several running events. These all attract athletes at the top of their game but, perhaps, none as famous as Deeside's own Donald Dinnie.

Dinnie, who was born in Aboyne, was an all-round, professional athlete, beating all-comers in strength and speed competitions. He competed in 16 Highland Games, excelling in sprint, hurdles, long and high jump, the hammer throw and tossing the caber. His career, which included Strongman tours of America, spanned more than 50 years during which he won 11,000 competitions. Dinnie was still performing as a strongman in his seventies. Little wonder, then, that he was proclaimed the nineteenth century's greatest athlete and was inducted into the Scottish Hall of Fame in 2002.

Above: Throwing the hammer at the Ballater Highland Games.

In the days before out-of-town retail outlets and online supermarket deliveries, the local shop was where villagers did much of their day-to-day shopping. It was one of the three key ingredients of the community – the other two being the pub and the church – and provided a valuable sociable and commercial hub; a place to chat to neighbours while you picked up a paper and a pint of milk.

As shopping habits changed, however, rents increased and post offices closed, and increasing numbers of village shops closed down too. According to the Rural Shops Alliance, 2,500 have shut in the last decade, and 200 still close every year. In 2016 there were 12,000 village shops in the country, about 50 per cent fewer than a decade previously.

But the outlook is not entirely bleak: shopping habits continue to evolve and the big weekly shop at supermarkets is being replaced by smaller, more frequent top-up shops. This, together with an enthusiasm for shopping locally, has led to the reintroduction of the village store. Many sell bread, cheese, preserves and vegetables produced nearby, with neighbouring farms supplying meat, milk and eggs, which are sold alongside a variety of discounted goods.

This time around, village shops are able to survive financially because many are community-owned and manned by volunteers with profits going back into the community. Often they provide the only form of retail in isolated areas – handy for the elderly and less mobile – and offer additional services including free Wi-Fi, coffee and a place to pick up your parcels. There are other less quantifiable benefits, of course: they bring life into the heart of the village and are the place to have a chat and catch up on local news. Once the doors of the village shop reopen, the neighbourhood begins to come back to life.

NORTH YORKSHIRE

From Yorkshire puddings to parkin, Yorkshire tea, flat caps and whippets, there are many traditions associated with Yorkshire. Its villages have cleverly remained true to their past, drawing on these traditions, while using them as a foundation for the future. Customs are being boosted and revived, while a spirit of enterprise is creating new ones.

Historically, the county of Yorkshire was divided into three areas: East, West and North Ridings ('riding' is derived from an Old English word meaning 'third'). North Yorkshire encompasses most of North Riding and some of East and West. It is the biggest county in England, and most of the Yorkshire Dales, all of the North York Moors and 800 villages lie within its boundaries. Its magnificent and unpopulated landscape (40 per cent of the county comprises national parks) has led to its moniker: 'God's Own County', a name often proudly declared by Yorkshire men and women.

Thwaite, Keld and Swaledale sheep

The Yorkshire Dales are characterised by ancient fields, drystone walls, fine stone buildings and plenty of sheep. Agriculture is still a driving force in the Swaledale village of Thwaite but these days tourism comes close as many walkers head for its rolling hills and tumbling streams.

The relatively unchanged, isolated pockets of farming communities like Thwaite have kept the local dialect alive. The best preserved of any dialect in England, it is also said to be very similar to Viking speech. ('Thwaite', for example, is derived from an old Scandinavian word meaning 'clearing', 'meadow' or 'paddock'.)

Above: The stone houses of Thwaite overlooking the stream, Thwaite Beck.

Isolated villages like Thwaite are often the places to find dialects that have been relatively untempered by the passing of time. Throughout the UK, these are rich and varied, often differing in the same county. The Yorkshire Dialect Society points out that there is no single Yorkshire dialect but a variety of speech patterns across the region. The accent most associated with the county and heard on TV and radio dramas hails from the more industrialised areas but the traditional speech as spoken in rural communities sounds quite different and has a strong Scandinavian influence.

Words used in contemporary Yorkshire
Baht: without (as in, 'On Ilkla Moor baht 'at')
Cat hawed: drunk
Lap: to cover or wrap up
Lowance: a packed lunch; from 'allowance'
Lug: ear
Mash: to brew, as in tea
Nowt: nothing
Owt: anything
Rive: to tear or rip out
Skeltered: crooked
Slape: slippery
Urchin: hedgehog
Yam: home

For more words, visit www.yorkshiredialectsociety.org.uk

YORKSHIRE DALES

A land of narrow valleys and attractive villages, of heather-covered hills and moors, of ancient abbeys and castles, the principal dales are readily accessible by rail and form a holiday paradise for walkers, anglers and all who prefer the quieter place

Train services and fares from BRITISH RAILWAYS **stations, offices and agencies**

Take the many different words ascribed to that valuable local resource: sheep. Swaledale ewes, as farmed in Thwaite and the nearby village of Keld, are distinctive creatures with off-white wool, white around their noses and eyes, and curled horns. Their thick coats make them particularly suited to survival on the exposed Yorkshire Dales. As Keld is the highest village in the Dales, this is particularly useful.

The sheep farmers of Thwaite and Keld have bestowed different names on their sheep for different stages of their lives: from hoggs (9–18 months), to shearlings (a year old before its first shearing), to tups – sheep aged three years and above. This is just a small example of the rich vocabulary of the region.

Above: A farmer and his sheep stand beside a stream in the village of Muker.

Muker and the Silver Band

The village of Muker grew thanks to lead mining in the surrounding hills. It now boasts a pub, a parish church and even an art gallery. It is also home to one of the last surviving silver bands in Swaledale. The Muker Silver Band was formed to celebrate Queen Victoria's Diamond Jubilee and made its first public appearance on Jubilee Day, 22 June 1897. For 50 years the band was exclusively male – comprising mostly young farmers – and played at village events. The members were self-taught, played a simple repertoire and did not compete in competitions. These days, more than a third of the band consists of women and they play over 20 concerts a year. Most Swaledale villages had their own bands but Muker's is one of the few to survive, thanks to the dedication and enthusiasm of its village community.

Since the Industrial Revolution of the early 19th century, brass and silver bands have been part of the fabric of Yorkshire life. Many collieries had their own brass band – the first civilian band in the world was the Stalybridge Old Band formed in 1809 – and competitions became popular (and fiercely contested) by the 1850s. One of the more famous is the Grimethorpe Colliery Band (as featured in the 1996 film *Brassed Off*). Larger factories also sponsored bands: the Black Dyke Mills Band being one example. Despite the closure of the collieries and subsequent lack of funding, the tradition continues, although finding the money to pay for and maintain instruments can be a challenge. Village bands, like the one in Muker, were originally linked to a local factory but are now mostly independent. None of the players are paid so the survival of the band depends on community spirit and good will. Large or small, brass and silver bands have certain instruments in common: cornets, flugelhorns, tenor horn, baritone horn, bass trombone, euphonium, bass and percussion. The size of the band is generally between 27 and 29 players though often there are fewer.

And if you were wondering what the difference between a brass and silver band is, the word 'silver' hails from the time when brass instruments were cheaper than silver-plated ones. A silver band was considered more successful – in other words richer – than a brass band. Although costs now are similar, some bands continue to carry the name.

Grassington and the Calendar Girls

Little did the ladies of Grassington Women's Institute realise that their modest fundraising scheme would propel them to international stardom. The story of the naked calendar modelled by members of the WI has become legendary, and was turned into a film, a stage play and a musical. But how did it all begin?

When one of the WI ladies, Tricia, suggested that members pose for a nude calendar as an alternative to the usual ones featuring bridges and churches, the idea was dismissed as a joke. That was until a friend of the WI and one of the member's husbands, John Baker, was diagnosed with cancer in 1998 and died soon afterwards. The WI ladies wanted to come up with a project that would keep his wife Angela busy through the winter and so they revived the calendar idea. Terry Logan, the husband of another member, Linda Logan, and an artist, stepped up to take the pictures. Despite their initial nerves, the ladies stripped off and struck poses (with strategically placed props) that represented different aspects of the WI: from jam making to tea drinking and cake baking. They thought they would raise a few hundred pounds, but once the calendar was published the publicity and the fundraising didn't stop – so far the WI has raised nearly £4 million for leukaemia and lymphoma research – and the amount keeps rising.

Right: The original Calendar Girls.

40

Goathland and the Long Sword Dance

Surrounded by heather on the high, wild expanse of the North York Moors, Goathland is a true moorland community. It will be familiar to anyone who watched *Heartbeat*, the TV police drama set in 1960s Yorkshire: Goathland was the setting for the fictional village of Aidensfield. Landmarks from the programme are still recognisable, from the village stores, to the pub and the railway station.

But traditions in Goathland stretch back much further than the 1960s. It is one of the few villages left keeping the Long Sword Dance alive. This is thanks to the Goathland Plough Stots, a traditional long sword team, revived in 1922 after a lapse of 40 years. It is believed that the sword dance began with the Vikings who used it to encourage their gods to bring a rich harvest but its origins are murky. Each dance requires six sword dancers accompanied by the Gentleman, Old Isaac, the Fool and fiddle and accordion players. Keith Thompson, who is president of the Plough Stots, plays the Fool and has done so for 25 years. The dance ends with all six swords locked together in a geometric shape that resembles a star.

The Goathland Plough Stots dance throughout the year, not just in Goathland, but also in other villages. As more of us become interested in native traditions and customs, they represent our ancient and symbolic past.

Above: The scenic railway station at Goathland, now used for steam trains.

Brompton-by-Sawdon and the birth of aviation

Sheep are right at home on the North York Moors: it is said that they can walk for 25 miles (40.2km) without leaving the heather, and there are few people or cars to trouble them. But it is not all wide-open landscape up here – narrow valleys have carved their way into the plateau and, on the sheltered south side, dozens of small communities have sprung up.

Brompton-by-Sawdon is one such village which, despite its remote location, has a remarkable claim to fame: this was where aviation was born. Brompton Hall on the edge of the village was once the home of Sir George Cayley, sixth baronet and owner of 9,000 acres (3,642 acres). A keen engineer, when he wasn't managing his estate he was in his workshop – inventing. We can thank Sir George for the theatre safety curtain, self-righting lifeboats, seat belts, an artificial hand and automatic braking on trains, among other things.

Above left: A view across the pond to the church at Brompton-by-Sawdon.
Above right: The reconstructed Cayley man carrier of 1853 photographed in towed flight in 1973.

But, perhaps most notably, he invented the world's first successfully flown, heavier than air, aircraft. Since his schooldays, Sir George had been obsessed with the idea of flight. He studied birds for over 50 years and developed theories of aerodynamic lift and stability leading to the creation of a glider or, as he called it, his governable parachute. In 1853 he tested his invention, manned by his coachman, in front of a handful of staff and the local sheep. The glider flew about 600–900ft (183–274m), the coachman was shaken up (he disembarked with the words, 'Please Sir George, I wish to give notice. I was hired to drive and not to fly'), and the story of flight was launched.

George Cayley didn't patent any of his inventions and made no money from them whatsoever. The purpose of his work was to benefit mankind. He also brought glory to this small patch of Yorkshire.

Ravenscar: the village that never was

The advent of the railways in the 1800s saw large numbers of Victorians heading to the coast to indulge in a new phenomenon, the British seaside holiday. On the North Yorkshire coast, Whitby turned from fishing to tourism and Scarborough, which already attracted visitors to its spa, built the Grand Hotel, one of the largest hotels in Europe.

Further along the coast, plans were in place to turn a village called Peak into the next seaside destination. A London property developer bought the land, renamed the village Ravenscar and set about selling his dream. Potential investors, enticed by a glossy poster that promised splendid seaside living, paid a deposit of £1, 16 shillings for an £18 plot. Sewers and pavements were laid but although large numbers reserved a plot, fewer than 50 houses were built (the plan was to build thousands), and none as a result of off-plan sales.

Ravenscar may have had sea views but the problem was that the beach was 600ft (183m) below at the foot of a cliff. As soon as plotholders got wind of the inaccessibility of their coastal dream, they withdrew from the purchase and Ravenscar was left an undeveloped dream.

Above: A poster produced for the London & North Eastern Railway (LNER) to promote rail travel to the Yorkshire Dales.

Great Ayton and Captain Cook

This village at the northern end of the North York Moors has been a centre for weaving, tanning, brewing and tile making but is best known as the former home of Captain James Cook. This true Yorkshire hero lived in the village from the age of eight until 16. His parents were farmworkers at Aireyholme Farm, which still exists today. What has vanished, though, is the cottage that the Cook family lived in. This was sold to Australia in 1933 and dismantled stone by stone to be re-erected in Melbourne as a lasting memorial to the man who 'discovered' the south-east of the country in 1770. Not all the villagers were happy to see the cottage go – the butcher pinched a stone and hid it in a wall. Ironically, it might not even have been Cook's home: local wisdom says it was actually his parents' retirement home. A recent theory based on a photo from the 1930s suggests a new location, and the villagers are busy working with an archaeologist to excavate the site. Artefacts found during the dig indicate that it is the right period for an 18th-century building, and perimeter walls and the remains of a fire have also been uncovered. Another stone or two to sell to the Australians, perhaps?

Staithes: A village full of artists

The village of Staithes is delightful confusion of cottages and alleyways formed by landscape, economy and history. The red-roofed houses cling to the cliffs, appearing to tumble towards the sea and an unusually large harbour. The young James Cook got his first taste of the sea here when he moved to Staithes from Great Ayton aged 16, to work as an assistant to a greengrocer.

By the 1880s, Staithes had become one of the most important fishing villages on the Yorkshire coast. The harbour was filled with 'cobbles', the word for classic Staithes boats with sleek, Viking-ship lines. Local people depended on the sea for their livelihoods – a precarious and dangerous way of life.

In 1894, the picturesque houses, narrow alleys and busy harbour drew a collection of artists known as the Staithes Group to the village. Inspired by French Impressionists, they painted *en plein air* (outdoors), recording the architecture, fishermen and coastal landscape. Between 20 and 30 artists settled here, forming a group led by Dame Laura Knight and her husband Harold. Their paintings are a record of life in the village at the time: a lost world of fishermen, boats and hard work, albeit in a particularly lovely setting. This artistic spirit is still very much alive in Staithes today with many artists living here, or visiting, and showing their work in the village's galleries.

Above: Captain Cook, Great Ayton's famous resident.

Right: The harbour at Staithes.

CUMBRIA

Whether it's the wide-open sweep of Morecambe Bay, the towering presence of Blencathra or the string of beautiful, much-loved lakes, in Cumbria the landscape always dominates.

Predominantly rural and relatively uninhabited (apart from during the summer season when it is inundated with tourists), the county incorporates the Lake District and the Lake District National Park, an Area of Outstanding Natural Beauty and inspiration for writers and artists, including John Ruskin, William Wordsworth and Beatrix Potter.

Coniston: Two very different vessels

A few miles from the ever-popular Lake Windermere but less busy, Coniston Lake is the third longest in the Lake District. Surrounded by mountains and forests, it is a serene spot – it's hard to imagine that it once boomed with the noise of heavy industry from copper mining. These days it is all calm water and noble fells.

The Gondola

It is particularly peaceful out on the lake cruising on the Gondola, a Victorian steam-powered yacht. The Gondola was originally launched in 1859 to carry passengers, mainly tourists, from the Furness and Coniston Railways further

Below: Autumnal colours reflected in the water at Coniston.

along the lake. Modelled on Venetian boats, it was described in the company's brochure as 'a perfected combination of the Venetian gondola and the English steam yacht – having the elegance, comfort and speed of the latter, and the graceful lightness and quiet gliding motion of the former.'

The Gondola was in service until 1936, after which time it was used as a houseboat, and then fell into disrepair, spending more than a decade submerged in the lake. Fortunately, in 1979, the National Trust raised funds to restore it and, with a new hull, boiler and superstructure, it is back on the water. Passengers can now cruise elegantly around the lake, enjoying the views and appreciating the handsome details of the interior.

Bluebird

A less tranquil voyage was undertaken by Donald Campbell in 1967. Campbell had broken the water speed record four times on Coniston Lake between 1956 and 1959. He returned to Coniston, surrounded by engineers, officials, the press and many fans in November 1966, determined to break the magic barrier of 300mph (483km/h). His core team stationed themselves at Coniston for months, waiting for the ideal conditions: the weather had to be right and Bluebird, his boat, had to be in perfect working order.

Campbell waited and tinkered with Bluebird for two months, even taking the boat out on Christmas day. Then, on 4 January 1967, everything seemed to come together. It was a crisp, frosty morning and the lake was flat and calm. Campbell approached a speed of 320mph (515km/h) very quickly but as he turned the boat around to come back down the lake, it lost stability, flipped over and crashed back into the water.

Donald Campbell died in the accident and his body was not discovered until 2001. Although he wasn't a local man by birth, he has become part of Coniston's story. Bluebird is currently being restored and will return to the village – Campbell's family have made it clear that the boat and its pilot belong here.

Above: Donald Campbell in his boat, Bluebird, on the lake at Coniston.

Many British children have grown up reading Beatrix Potter's tales of country animals and their adventures on and off the cabbage patch. Not many realise, however, that she was a champion of the countryside and actively involved in its conservation, particularly in the Lake District, where she lived for most of her life.

Using an inheritance from an aunt, in 1905 Beatrix Potter bought Hill Top Farm in the village of Near Sawrey close to Windermere. She quickly learned how to raise livestock, eventually adding sheep. She was especially interested in the indigenous Herdwick sheep because of their ability to thrive on high fells and in harsh, bleak places, and because they constantly crop the grass and keep invasive species at bay. Despite this, the sheep and their farmers were under threat from forestry plantation, tourism and other developments associated with modern life. Beatrix, determined to protect their future, bought another farm and restored its land with thousands of Herdwick sheep.

When she died, she left her farms to the National Trust on condition they maintained Herdwick flocks. Not only has the National Trust continued to do this, but it has also introduced Herdwicks to its land in other parts of the country.

Threlkeld and how its people tried to buy a mountain

At over 2,800ft (868m) Blencathra (also known as Saddleback) is one of the giants of the Lakes and a favourite with fell walkers. So when its owner, Hugh Lowther, the 8th Earl of Lonsdale, put it up for sale in 2014 to pay an inheritance bill, local people were concerned that it might be bought by someone who didn't have its best interests at heart. A campaign, starting as a Facebook group, began to raise funds to buy the mountain. It wasn't long before more than £250,000 was raised, a great deal of money but not enough (it was on the market for £1.75m).

Two years after first putting Blencathra up for sale, Lowther settled his bill by selling a painting and decided not to sell the land. The Friends of Blencathra continued to fight to buy it but finally admitted defeat in September 2016.

Below: A cloud-shrouded Blencathra, with the ancient Castlerigg Stone Circle in the foreground.

Kirkoswald and hound trailing

Kirkoswald is one of a number of sandstone villages dotted along the bottom of the lush, winding Eden Valley. It has been an important settlement since the 12th century and its name derives from King Oswald of Northumbria who, 500 years earlier, helped to spread Christianity across the north of England. Hound trailing may not date back that far but it has been taking place in the village for over 200 years.

This sociable and lively event involves a lot of whistle blowing and cheering as a large number of dogs (there are 500 on the circuit) race across moorland, fields and fells in pursuit of a trail made from a mixture of paraffin and oil of aniseed laid by trailers dragging rags. The course is 5 miles (8km) long and takes the dogs around 20 minutes to complete. This is just enough time for owners and spectators to lay bets – as soon as the dogs approach the finishing line the betting stops.

There are few other places in the country where farmers and landowners would allow dozens of hounds to tear across their land. This is a Cumbrian tradition made for the Cumbrian landscape.

Right: A huntsman with a pack of Fell Hounds, used for trailing.

Nenthead: A mining community

The eastern extremity of Cumbria as it climbs up into the Pennines, is rugged, bleak and inhospitable. So it is somewhat surprising that the village of Nenthead was built up here, in the hills, at 1,500ft (457m) above sea level. It becomes less of a puzzle, however, when you learn that this is a rich mining area. Mining has taken place here since medieval times and boomed in the middle of the 18th century when the demand for lead soared as increasing numbers of houses were built with lead roofs and pipes.

The Quaker-owned London Lead Company owned and ran the mines and realised that the miners and their families needed decent places to live. In response, they created Nenthead – one of the country's first purpose-built industrial villages. By 1861, 2,000 people lived in Nenthead, and the progressive and benevolent Quakers also built a market hall, school, a wash house and public baths to cater for their needs. They built a working men's reading room – now a community shop but then a precursor to a library (the Public Libraries Act of 1850 was the first step in the creation of free public libraries throughout the UK but these took many years to establish) – and installed electric street lighting from excess power generated by the mines.

The Methodist Chapel was built in 1873 and still dominates the village although it hasn't been used for worship since 2002. However, the village community has plans to buy it and turn it into a café, move the community shop here and use the generous amounts of space for concerts and recitals.

Above: The entrance to Nenthead Mines.

Large, plain chapel buildings are found at the heart of many British villages, especially those in mining areas. These Methodist chapels were built from 1760–1820 when missionaries spread the faith through the country, particularly in working-class areas, such as North Yorkshire, Wales and Cornwall (see page 177).

Methodism was driven by two brothers – John and Charles Wesley – during the 18th century. John preached directly to disenfranchised Anglicans in fields, collieries and churchyards, attracting crowds of thousands. John Wesley warned against the dangers of alcohol and gambling and many Methodists were teetotallers. Although Methodism is not as widespread now, its legacy remains in the hard-working principles of mining villages and in its handsome and almost indestructible chapels.

Cartmel and sticky toffee pudding

When the Lake District National Park was created in 1951, Cartmel was left a few hundred yards outside the boundary, but this doesn't mean it has been ignored. A couple of surprising things have kept it in the public eye.

The village grew up around the 12th-century Priory of St Mary and St Michael, which looks down upon its pretty cluster of houses and village square. The Priory is architecturally and historically remarkable. As the Bastford guide puts it: 'From without it strikes the eye at once by reason of the curious diagonal set of the upper part of the tower upon the lower. It is certainly an enrichment of shape without any sacrifice of symmetry.'

One of the buildings by the Priory – the village shop – is responsible for Cartmel's latest claim to fame: it is the home of sticky toffee pudding. Jean and Howard John started the business in 1989 when they bought the post office and general store opposite the Priory. They started making sticky toffee pudding from a family recipe and, working with daughter Sarah and son-in-law David, sales took off until the pudding became a sizeable business. Eventually they shut the post office and just concentrated on the puddings, which are now dispatched all over the world. Customers can also buy the irresistible and gooey puddings to take away or order online. The family puts the secret to their success down to good-quality ingredients – 'proper butter, free-range eggs, nice dark sugar' – and the branding which has proved a big PR hit for the business and the village.

The village's other culinary success story is a Michelin-starred restaurant, hailed as one of Britain's finest. In 2003 Simon Rogan, a Hampshire chef, took a punt and opened his restaurant L'Enclume housed in the old village smithy. Right from the start he was determined to use only local ingredients – the meat comes from local producers and the vegetables come from Rogan's own 12-acre (4.9ha) farm just outside the village. Here he grows all the vegetables that flourish in the Cumbrian climate, including lettuce, turnips, shallots, kale and leeks and this informs all his menu choices. Little wonder then that the restaurant has led the way in making the Lake District a food-lover's destination.

Above: The iconic sticky toffee pudding.

Below: Walkers on the beach at Morecambe Bay at evening time.

Arnside and Morecambe Bay

Perched prettily over the upper reaches of Morecambe Bay, Arnside is the last village in Cumbria before you cross into Lancashire. It first became popular in the mid-19th century when the new railway line brought day-trippers and holiday-makers and in the summer, when the bunting is out and visitors stroll along the promenade and the pier, it is the quintessential seaside resort. Bucket and spaders get more than they bargain for, however, when the tide goes out, and Morecambe Bay's 120 sq. miles (310 sq. km) of sand is revealed.

This vast stretch of sand is far more treacherous than it looks – although it appears firm and inviting, there are stretches of quicksand everywhere. A spring tide takes just 1½ hours to flow in and can easily catch you unawares. Many an unfortunate person or animal has become stuck out there as the tide hurtles in at up to 15mph (24.1km/h). Fortunately, a team of 22 volunteers who make up Bay Search and Rescue, are on constant alert. They come to the aid of farm animals that have strayed from their grazing, disorientated walkers and vehicles mired in the quicksand, and on average, are called to action once a fortnight: a very reassuring and worthwhile service.

Grasmere and the Wordsworths

The Batsford guide describes the arterial road that runs north to south alongside Lake Windermere to Grasmere as 'the tourist's way'. The beauty of the scenery with its lakes and mountains has meant that it has always attracted visitors, especially in the summer, but there is another reason they come: the poet William Wordsworth who lived in Grasmere with his sister Dorothy.

These days, the village is given over to tourism with its granite and slate buildings housing art shops, cafés and a gingerbread shop, but not everyone is a fan of its Victorian architecture. Doreen Wallace, author of the Batsford guide dismissed it thus: 'The houses of the 19th-century influx of gentry and near gentry are loathly. Everything is wrong with them. The colour of this new slate has no mellowness, the roofs are harsh and cold, and wide gables? The screlly bits of wooden edging here and there look nearly meretricious. Bow windows abound, about 75 per cent are adorned with bamboo tables and aspidistras.'

Fortunately, Wordsworth had fewer qualms. He was 29 when he arrived in the village in 1799 and stayed here for the rest of his life – he is buried in the churchyard alongside Dorothy. They lived at the edge of the village in Dove Cottage, a simple home with a beautiful hillside garden that Wordsworth described as 'The loveliest spot that man hath ever found.' Although they went on to move to three further properties to cater for William's growing family, it is Dove Cottage that everyone remembers. Even during his lifetime, it had become a tourist attraction – Wordsworth was a popular poet and drew visitors hoping to see him or have a look around the garden, much like tourists of today.

Above: Dove Cottage, home of William Wordsworth.

Right: Lake Windermere, scenic even on a cloudy day.

WALES AND
THE NORTH WEST

Bounded by the Peak District and the Pennines, the North West is a mixture of thrilling landscape, industrial heritage and urban sprawl.

Anglesey, Wales's largest island, feels far away no matter where you live. Centuries ago it was even more remote, a forbidding outcrop that took determination to get to, along bumpy carriageways and then by ferry. Fortunately for us, in 1826 a suspension bridge designed by engineer Thomas Telford (dubbed the Colossus of Roads because of his work improving access to Scotland with a road network), was constructed across the Menai Strait linking the mainland to the island.

Wales

According to Batsford guide: 'The Menai Strait is so narrow that one is apt to forget that Anglesey is an island yet an island it is and whether one reaches it by Telford's mighty suspension bridge or by Stephenson's ringing tubular bridge, there is all the anticipation of a primitive sea-girt land.'

Before Telford's bridge was built, farmers on Anglesey would have had to swim the cattle across the often-turbulent water to take them to market. Stephenson's tubular bridge was built nearly 25 years later. It was all but

Below: Poster produced for London, Midland & Scottish Railway (LMS) showing the Britannia Tubular Bridge over the Menai Strait to Anglesey.

destroyed by fire in 1970 and was rebuilt as a box girder bridge to carry rail and road traffic. Driving over the bridge is a delight in itself and the perfect way to approach its lovely villages.

Below left: Traditional Welsh folk dancers performing outside the railway station with the longest name.
Below: Penmon Point Lighthouse on Anglesey.

Llanfairpwllgwyngyllgogerychwyrndrobwllllantysiliogogogoch

The famously long, and for most people, unpronounceable, name of this village in Anglesey is an early example of a PR stunt. The arrival of the railways in the 1860s prompted a local tailor, who was also something of a poet, to embellish the existing name Llanfair Pwllgwyngyll into the longest name of any railway station in Britain (in fact it is the longest in Europe and second longest one-word place name in the world). The aim was to entice trains to stop at the village, which indeed it did. It also brought many new visitors to the tiny rural community (the population then was just 300 – now it has grown to 3,000), who come to have their photograph taken beside the name on the station.

In case you're wondering, the village name translates as 'The parish church of St Mary (Llanfair) in Hollow (pwll) of the White Hazel (gwyn gyll) near the rapid whirlpool (y chwyrn drobwll) and the parish church of St Tysilio (Lantysilio) with a red cave (gogogoch)'.

Cemaes, Wylfa Nuclear Power Station and a garden

The pretty village of Cemaes, the most northerly village in Wales, clusters around its sheltered harbour and two sandy beaches. Once a busy port, it now attracts walkers on the Anglesey coastal path, fishermen and anyone who appreciates its Victorian seaside charm.

Just west of Cemaes, you will find a less lovely structure – Wylfa Nuclear Power Station – the only one in Wales. Construction began in 1963 and it has been in operation since 1971, a time when nuclear energy was regarded as a safe and renewable form of energy. Since then not only has it supplied energy for the local community and beyond, but it has provided work for the local people. The main Magnox reactors are now being decommissioned, but there are plans to build another station on the same site with the aim of supplying electricity within the first half of the 2020s.

The site of the power station was once part of a grand estate, Cestyll House, which was bought by the Hon. William Walter Vivian as a gift for his niece the Hon. Violet Vivian, daughter of Lord Vivian of Bodmin, Cornwall, in 1918. The house has been demolished but the pocket of lush greenery that is its garden remains and flourishes.

Violet Vivian was maid of honour to Queen Alexandra and a close personal friend of the Princess Victoria. Cestyll, and especially the garden, became an escape for her and her family far away from the confines and formality of court. Violet was instrumental in the creation of the garden, aided by Princess Victoria who engaged help from the Royal Gardens at Kew, which provided some of the plants. Despite its remote location, the garden drew some very eminent visitors, which caused quite a stir in the village.

The garden wraps around the Cafnan River and follows it to the sea. Violet made the most of the difficult site and planted white rhododendrons, maples, camellias, azaleas and clematis, all sheltered by a plantation of fir trees.

The garden opens to the public for three days each year over the May Bank Holiday weekend. However, with the plans for a new power station and changes in land ownership, there is some uncertainty about its future.

Right: A traditional whitewashed Welsh fishermans cottage in Cemaes.

Llanberis, sheep and the Snowdon Mountain Railway

In the 19th century, an explosion of pits, mines and quarries saw new communities in Wales spring up almost overnight. The country was transformed into the engine of the Empire, with the south dominated by coal mines, and the north becoming the slate capital of the world with one village at its heart: Llanberis. Although it is scenically placed – perched on the side of Lake Padarn and at the foot of Snowdon – slate mining prompted this damning review in the Batsford guide: 'The road into Llanberis is the way into the heart of the Snowdon forest, though much of it is an ordeal. For the new Llanberis is as ugly as sin, the glistening coal black slate piles falling sheer into Lake Padarn.' The slate industry was a major employer locally – 3,000 people worked here – and its two quarries covered over 700 acres (283ha). But eventually competition from cheaper roofing materials saw demand for slate decline sharply and the quarries closed in 1969.

Although this is an industrial village, built for business with rows of terraced houses, it is still a popular tourist spot and this is because of the Snowdon Mountain Railway. Built in 1896, the train takes passengers 4¾ miles (7.6km) from the village, and 3,560ft (1,085m) up to the summit of Snowdon. The spectacular, wrap-around view from the highest peak in England and Wales feels a world away from the slate piles below.

The lost village of Llanwddyn

Lake Vyrnwy in Powys lies serenely in the Vyrnwy valley, a popular destination for birdwatchers, cyclists and walkers. But its tranquil waters hold a secret: a few hundred yards from the shore lies the remains of the village of Llanwddyn. The reservoir was created to supply fresh, clean water to the city of Liverpool, 60 miles (96.6km) away. When construction of a dam started in 1881, before the valley was flooded, the 37 houses, three inns and two chapels were demolished. The villagers whose families had lived there for generations were displaced but not homeless: the Liverpool Corporation rebuilt the village on the edge of the reservoir and most, but not all, of them moved in. The dam took ten years to build and provided work for over 1,000 people. When it was completed in 1891 it was the largest man-made reservoir in Europe.

Above: Snowdon Mountain Railway, with a train making its way through the hills.

Left: Lake Vyrnwy, photographed in late autumn.

Portmeirion

Traditionally, villages expand and develop over the years, reflecting periods of decline and growth. As the Bastford guide says: 'A village is but rarely a deliberate work of art, and it does not, like a painting or a piece of sculpture, owe its existence and character to an individual will.'

There are, however, a few exceptions, and Portmeirion on the North Wales coast is one of the most notable. The village is the brainchild of one man – the architect Clough Williams-Ellis – who bought what was a beautiful but neglected wilderness in 1925 for £20,000, and transformed it into a pastel-coloured coastal village. Reminiscent of fishing villages around the Mediterranean, Portmeirion is a pretty jumble of elegant and fanciful buildings (some salvaged from demolition sites) overlooking the sea and backed by hanging woodland.

The village has no permanent inhabitants – everyone here is either on holiday or tending to visitors' needs. It is a place conceived for pleasure and delight: the perfect holiday destination. Clough Williams-Ellis wanted it to be alive, to give joy and to inspire writers, painters, artists and musicians. He succeeded in his wish: writers including George Bernard Shaw, H. G. Wells and Noël Coward, who wrote *Blithe Spirit* in the hotel, all stayed here.

These days the fun and inspiration continues with visitors staying in its hotels and cottages or simply visiting for the day. The annual music Festival No.6 (whose name comes from the cult TV programme *The Prisoner*, which was filmed in Portmeirion) also attracts wide-ranging and interesting acts that the village's founder would surely have approved of and enjoyed.

Above: Colourful buildings in Portmeirion, built in the Italian style.

The North West

Lancashire's supremacy during the Industrial Revolution at the start of the 19th century saw it become one of the wealthiest regions in the country. For a time it was the world's cotton-making machine and mills couldn't be built quickly enough. This produced a very different style of village; the ramshackle charm of stone cottages was replaced by terrace upon terrace of workers' houses that were centered not around the grand hall of a feudal lord or local aristocrat, but the new employer – the mill.

Wycoller and the ruin of Wycoller Hall

There was a time when the pretty village of Wycoller looked as though it was to be left abandoned and uninhabited. At the start of the 19th century, it had a population of more than 350, but a 100 years later, only one household remained. The village had been a sheep-farming community and during the 18th century, the cottages hummed with the sound of spinning and weaving wool. The roads rattled with the clatter of the weavers' clogs – it is said that the grooves in one of the village's bridges, the Clapper Bridge, were worn by the weavers' clogs.

However, the advent of power looms, meant that the weavers had to look for work elsewhere, and moved away to find it in the big mills in nearby towns and cities. Then, in 1890, there were plans to create a reservoir to provide water for industry in the Colne Valley by damming Wycoller Beck that runs through the village. Fortunately, when a natural source of water was found, those plans came to nothing and the village was saved. Even so, more people drifted away and eventually the entire village was bought by the local water board and continued to decline. Redemption came via a local conservation group, The Friends of Wycoller, which started a campaign to conserve it in 1950. Now it is a flourishing community once more and many of the old buildings have a new purpose – the 18th-century barn is now a Visitor Centre, and the village has a café and craft centre – and it has been the proud recipient of a Britain in Bloom award for Best Kept Village.

A major part of the Friends campaign has been to restore as much as they could of Wycoller Hall, the magnificent ruin at the heart of the village. Built in the 16th century, it was once the fine and prosperous estate of the Cunliffe family. Legend has it that it was the inspiration for Charlotte Brontë's depiction of Ferndean Manor in *Jane Eyre*. The Brontës lived nearby in Howarth, so that could well be the case.

In the early 19th century, however, Wycoller Hall fell victim to its owner's debts and was sold and divided up between creditors, with much of the stonework being sold to build a cotton mill. The building survived but only as an unoccupied ruin. The ruined Hall is a romantic and atmospheric (reputedly haunted) place to visit and the village, with its seven bridges and stone houses, is as typically Lancastrian as you can get.

THE PANOPTICON 'ATOM'

On the hill above Wycoller in Wycoller Country Park, is a curious modern structure that looks as if it has been deposited by aliens. This is Pendle's Panopticon 'Atom', a ferro-cement structure coated with metallic paint, which not only provides somewhere to shelter but is also a place to view the surrounding landscape through its circular windows. 'Atom', designed by Peer Meacock, Andrew Edmunds and Katarina Novomestska of Peter Meacock Projects, is one of four panopticons in East Lancashire. Each one is a startling piece of art that not only frames the landscape, but also embellishes it, being both viewpoint and landmark.

Harle Syke, Lancashire, and clog dancing

Throughout history, people have always moved to where they can
find work, and the lure of industry created whole new communities.
Harle Syke, once a quiet sheep-farming community, became part of
Lancashire's domination of the cotton industry when, in 1850, the
first cotton mill and row of workers' cottages were built. The village
expanded steadily until seven mills run by 11 weaving firms were in
operation. Workers were attracted to Harle Syke and other villages
across Lancashire by the promise of a roof over their heads and
guaranteed work.

Above: Queen Street Mill, on the outskirts of

Burnley, which was built in 1894.

Right: Brick mill chimneys in Harle Syke.

At one point, there were 1,000 looms clattering away in one mill, providing long, hard and dangerous work for the whole family including children who, from the age of nine, went to school in the morning and worked in the mill in the afternoon.

Today all the looms are quiet and the mill buildings have found other uses as industrial units and an antique centre. Queen Street Mill was converted to a textile museum after it closed in 1982 but that too has shut due to lack of funding.

The spirit of the mills lives on though, through the feet of the local people. Clog dancing is alive and kicking, and the streets still resonate with the sounds of these wooden shoes mimicking the rhythms of the looms and the workers who operated them (see page 78).

Alderley Edge

In the early twentieth century a decline in industry and agriculture saw people forced to leave their rural communities in search of work. For a while, it looked as though Britain's villages would vanish – until an unlikely saviour arrived – the motor car. In the 1960s, with increased car ownership, many villages were reborn as suddenly people could commute to work.

Alderley Edge, which is 6 miles (9.7km) from Macclesfield and 15 miles (24.1km) from Manchester, has been perfectly positioned to meet the needs of commuters since 1842. That year, the Manchester and Birmingham Railway Company built a line to what was then Chorley, and offered Manchester mill owners free season tickets if they built houses within 1 mile (1.6km) of the station. Chorley was renamed Alderley Edge to avoid confusion with another railway station in Lancashire, and so began its elevation to a high-status village. The mill owners built grand houses on the hill and their servants took up residence in nearby cottages. A service industry of greengrocers, bakers and butchers sprung up around them and attracted more wealthy homeowners.

Today it is still the village of choice of the super-rich – but now this is footballers and soap stars rather than mill owners. Boutiques and nail bars are interspersed with cafés and restaurants and there is a general air of prosperity. At a time when so many villages are losing their shops, there is no denying that this one is thriving.

Right: A great sweep of Cheshire countryside can be seen from Alderley Edge.

Abbots Bromley, Staffordshire, and the Horn Dance

Every year on Wakes Monday, the day following Wakes Sunday – the first Sunday after 4 September – dancers gather at the church in Abbots Bromley at 8a.m. Six sets of reindeer antlers are taken from the wall and the festivities known as Horn Dance Day begin.

The origins of the Abbots Bromley Horn Dance Day are rather obscure and the original meaning has grown faint over the years. Some speculate that it

Above: Men and children gather for the dance in 2008.

started as a ritual to ensure a plentiful catch of deer (hence the horns), others that it is associated with the harvest and fertility. Whatever its original purpose, these days it brings the community together and attracts visitors keen to observe the spectacle.

The Batsford guide describes it succinctly: 'Twelve persons take part, six dressed to represent Robin Hood and his followers, the other six wearing reindeer horns. After dancing through the market place the six deer men are chased by the others out of town and along the boundaries of the parish ...'

The 12 dancers are accompanied by an accordion player, a Maid Marian (a man in a dress), a hobby horse, a fool and a couple of youngsters. This bunch of merry makers dances through, then out of the village to Blithfield Hall, owned by the Bagot family. The dance is an uncomplicated one due to the weight of the antlers, which interestingly date back to the 11th century, and may have come from Scandinavia. By 8pm the antlers are returned to the church but this does not stop the merrymaking, which continues into the night.

Above: The Horn Dance performed in the 1940s.
Above right: The festivities continue with accordion playing and beer.

Clog dance: Developed in Lancashire cotton mills where workers wore wooden-soled clogs, clog dancing was originally performed in towns and villages during the Industrial Revolution in the 19th century. Workers would tap out the rhythms of their machines in their clogs to keep their feet warm, holding competitions during their breaks judged on best rhythm patterns. Clog dancing became a proper staged competition and is still practiced in Lancashire, Cheshire, Yorkshire, Cumbria and Derbyshire.

Maypole dance: Dancing around a maypole holding a ribbon has become one of the symbols of Merrie England. The ritual dance takes place on 1 May and is performed by pairs of boys

and girls who stand alternately around the base of the pole, each holding the end of a ribbon. The boys go one way, the girls the other weaving the ribbons as they go, until they meet at the base.

Morris dancing: Although it is associated with the celebration of ancient Celtic festivals and rituals, Morris dancing almost died out in the late 19th century. Its revival was kick-started by folklorist Cecil Sharp in the early 20th century, and it exploded in popularity in the 1960s, when female teams also sprung up. Different villages have different customs and costumes, and some dancers hold handkerchiefs while others employ short sticks. The dancers are accompanied by musicians – often fiddle and accordion players. Morris dancing is still performed widely, in open air in villages in rural Britain, often during the Christmas period.

The Long Sword Dance: This dance using rigid metal or wooden swords is found scattered all over Yorkshire. There are variations in the numbers of dancers and in their steps, but each dance ends with the swords locked in a six-pointed star formation. Sword dances are often still performed by village teams such as the Goathland Plough Stots, see page 41.

PEMBROKESHIRE

The far south-west corner of Wales boasts a
spectacular coastline with sandy beaches, hidden coves
and pretty harbour villages. Beyond the shoreline lies
fertile farmland, estuaries, castles and dramatic hills
scattered with farming communities.

The Batsford guide describes the county poetically:
'These are the oldest lands in Wales, the ancient ribs
and earliest rocks of geological time, cut only by the
little streams down to the creeks of the coast.'

To see the county as a backwater, however,
would be a mistake. The Normans recognised its
unique location, with good trading links to Cornwall,
Devon and Ireland, and it is thought that William
the Conqueror himself visited. More recently, slate
quarrying, brick making, farming and tourism have
provided livelihoods for its people. Nowadays visitors
enjoy the unspoiled beauty of the Pembrokeshire Coast
National Park, and the region's secret villages tucked
away in valleys and beside estuaries.

Manorbier and its romantic castle

Few villages have as romantic a setting as Manorbier. Not only does it sit snugly in a cove above a sandy, dune-backed beach, but it has its very own ruined castle. Little wonder then that Virginia Woolf, George Bernard Shaw and Siegfried Sassoon loved it here and visited frequently.

Manorbier Castle, which has stood guard over the bay since the Normans stormed across Wales and took control in Pembrokeshire 900 years ago, dominates the tiny village. Currently in a state of well-managed ruination, it has witnessed just two minor skirmishes and is now the setting for weddings and the occasional opera, as well as a place for visitors to amble, admiring the castle and its gardens. Manorbier also provided the ideal, picturesque location for the BBC's adaptation of *The Chronicles of Narnia* and the film version of Dodie Smith's evocative, coming-of-age novel *I Capture the Castle*.

Manorbier Castle is owned by Dame Emily Naper who inherited it as a teenager from her mother. She in turn took it over, bucking the tradition of primogeniture where property is passed through the male line. This departure from the norm may well originate from the days when the king gifted grand houses (and castles) to his mistresses. As Dame Emily has no daughters this unusual custom may come to a halt with her unless, as she says, one of her sons has 'a wonderful mistress'.

Above: Manorbier Castle, the ideal location for films and TV adaptations.

Left: A summer day on the beach at Manorbier.

Llangwm and the fisherwomen of Cleddau Estuary

Upstream from Pembroke Dock, and tucked into the hidden world of the Cleddau Estuary, is a quaint little village of stone cottages with blooming gardens and doors festooned with rambling roses. All is not quite as it seems, however: Llangwm's delightful appearance belies its hard-working past.

The waters of the estuary and its fertile floodplains have provided rich pickings for villagers who farmed the land and fished its waters for oysters, herring and salmon. Men and women were both involved in the fishing industry and the women, dressed in traditional costume, would take baskets of fish to sell at Tenby 15 miles (24.1km) away. Look closely at the cottages and you can see evidence of earlier occupants: their names include Alberta's Cottage and Florence's Cottage.

This was a matriarchal society and the women were strong characters – some chose their own husbands and kept their maiden names. This female dominance is said to date back to the 12th century, when the Normans seized control of the area and settled it with hundreds of people from Flanders who they could control, unlike the troublesome Welsh. The story of the Flemish settlers, and their female bias, has been told in a 16½ft (5m) long tapestry, 'The Talking Tapestry of Langum', which was based on children's drawings stitched by local people and overseen by vicar and Master Weaver and Embroiderer Andrew Johnson. It now hangs in the village church. The village's Flemish legacy also lives on in a variety of words that are still spoken here – 'hunted' means 'agitated', for example, and 'caffle' means 'confused'.

Lawrenny: An unlikely defender of our shores

Thoughts of war and bombing are far from the minds of anyone walking on the footpath of the Pembrokeshire Coast National Park as it winds its way along the Cleddau Estuary through the village of Lawrenny. Sailing boats glide past Lawrenny Quay caught on the wind, and kayakers paddle by. All seems tranquil and untroubled.

However, it was a different picture in 1940. Pembroke Dock, 5 miles (8km) downstream, was one of the most heavily bombed communities in Britain. German U-boats were in the ascendency in the Atlantic and the Royal Navy was the last line of defence from invasion. Numerous small sea planes were catapulted from battleships to act as the navy's eyes in the sky, reporting on what lay out at sea.

Above: Llangwm cockle women habitually walked their wares to markets and fairs, often as far afield as Carmarthen.

Right: A colourful sunset above the River Cleddau in Lawrenny.

As the bombing of Pembroke Dock continued into October 1941, a squadron of trainee sea pilots was installed in safer waters at a camp in Lawrenny. Suddenly, the village was invaded by Royal Navy personnel, with student pilots spending two to three months inhabiting its Victorian castle. The squadron stayed for a couple of years and when they weren't training, held dances and film shows to which the local people were invited. The memory of it is still fresh for some, especially one local girl who married a trainee pilot.

Bosherston: A village with farming at its heart

South Pembrokeshire's cliffs and beaches tend to grab most of the headlines but farming has always been of paramount importance. Conditions are ideal for agriculture: there is a long growing season due to the coastline's proximity to the Gulf Stream; the land is level and free-draining; and the soil is rich and fertile. All of these factors mean that the land is easy to farm – Pembrokeshire is known for its early potatoes, for example, which thrive in the good soil and the long, frost-free spring.

The village of Bosherston is at the heart of this fecund landscape. It owes its existence to the Cawdor family who owned 16,000 acres (6,475ha) and built the village on its Stackpole Estate to house some of the workers. As well as managing the land for agriculture, between 1780 and 1860 the Cawdors created a magnificent park around their home, Stackpole Court. The house was demolished in 1963 but much of what they created remains and includes Bosherston Lakes, the result of damming a limestone valley, which they then filled with a floating carpet of glorious waterlilies.

During the Second World War, the Army requisitioned 6,000 acres (2,428ha) of the Stackpole Estate for tank-training exercises. Fifty land girls were also stationed around Bosherston to be part of the war effort, digging for corn and potatoes, milking cows and working the ploughs. They have become stitched

Above (left to right): The Church of St Michael's and All Angels in Bosherston; Land girls with a horse and hay cart during World War II.

into the area's rich farming history – 70 years later there are still over 2,000 farms in Pembrokeshire and more dairy cows than people.

Cwm Gwaun and the ancient history of the Preseli Hills

North Pembrokeshire is a wild and rugged place – its jagged mountains and wild moorland a contrast to the gentler lowlands of the south. The 13-mile (21km) range of the Preseli Hills that runs through it is sparsely populated now but there is much evidence of ancient habitation. The landscape is peppered with prehistoric sites, including burial chambers, stone circles and Iron Age hill forts, and famously, and remarkably, 4,500 years ago large pieces of bluestone were taken from the hills and transported all the way to Wiltshire to build Stonehenge stone circle.

Cwm Gwaun is tucked away in a lushly wooded valley, like a village that time forgot. Most of its farming community of 300 people speaks Welsh and all its members keep alive a peculiar custom – they celebrate New Year on 13 January. When the rest of the country adopted the Julian calendar and ditched the Gregorian one in 1752, the residents of Cwm Gwaun dug their heels in and refused to change. Now for New Year on 13 January, a day called Hen Galan, the children walk from house to house singing traditional Welsh songs and receive sweets and money in return.

Above: A view of Preseli Hills from Carningli in Newport.

Mynachlog-ddu and the Rebecca Riots

Unlike Cwm Gwaun, the village of Mynachlog-ddu has no valley to protect it. It sits on a plateau 656ft (200m) above sea level in the heart of the Preseli Hills. It is a true and tough hill-farming community with a spirited past.

Between 1839 and 1843, the villagers sparked a rebellion here that spread across much of South and Mid Wales. The Turnpike Tolls saw landowners charge farmers to move sheep and fertiliser along the roads. Farmers and agricultural workers, already battling with poor harvests and economic difficulties, viewed the tolls as unfair taxation and saw themselves as victims of 'tyranny and oppression'. As many farm workers were unable to vote, their only recourse was protest. The rebellion was led by a Mynachlog-ddu man, Twm Carnabwth, a towering figure (6ft 4in/1.93m) with red hair. To disguise his identity, he wore women's clothes when leading the attacks on the hated toll-booths. It is said that the clothes were borrowed from a large elderly woman called Rebecca as they were the only clothes that fitted him, but this is unproved – the wearing of women's clothes as a protest was already a symbol of Welsh rebellion.

The Rebecca Riots spread with other protestors dressing as women and attacking toll-gates. Although the riots had no immediate effect, and the toll-gates were rebuilt, they prompted several reforms and the uprising is remembered every summer in the village. The riots are brought to life once more as boys dressed as Rebeccas in girls' clothing rally outside the house where Twm Carnabwth planned his rebellion before 'attacking' a toll-gate in a re-enactment of the 19th-century protests.

St Dogmaels and an award-winning market

The River Teifi marks a natural boundary between Pembrokeshire and Ceredigion as it flows to the sea. Overlooking its estuary is St Dogmaels, one of the largest villages in the region. This is largely due to its 12th-century abbey, which was the heartbeat of the village until its dissolution in 1536. Now, in its shadow, is a modern replacement – a thriving market.

During the Middle Ages a village had to apply to the Crown for a market charter before it became a market town. Nowadays, things are less tightly controlled and markets spring up all over the place, although farmers' markets,

Above: The Rebecca Riots in 1843.

Below: A secluded farmhouse in St Dogmael's.

like the one at St Dogmael's, are closely regulated. Even though the market only started in 2009, it has already picked up a number of awards, including a BBC Food and Farming Award in 2016 for best market.

The market takes places every Tuesday from 9a.m.–1p.m. among the ruins of the Abbey, overlooking the millpond and the working water mill. As scenic spots go, few can beat it. The stallholders sell the best produce that the fertile land of Pembrokeshire can offer – longhorn beef, lamb and mutton from the Gwaun Valley, locally caught fish and shellfish, freshly baked bread, seasonal vegetables, chutneys, local cheeses and free-range eggs.

Cider and mead is also for sale: a nod to the village's monastic past. As the water was unfit to drink in the Middle Ages, the Abbey's monks made cider from their apples and mead from honey. This could have unfortunate results; during the 1400s a monk called Howl was reprimanded by the Bishop of St David for drinking far too much mead and consorting with women in the local pubs.

The flourishing farmers' market at St Dogmael's is the place to go to stock up on fresh produce, from locally grown vegetables to cheese, chutney, bread and meat. It is one of a network of farmers' markets that have sprung up in British towns and villages over the past 20 years as we have rediscovered the pleasures and benefits of buying directly from producers rather than pushing a trolley past rows of uniform vegetables and fruit in supermarkets.

Markets have always existed, of course – before the advent of greengrocers and supermarkets, they were the prime place to buy food. Farmers went to market to sell excess produce and to raise extra income but, as food became pre-packaged and imported, the popularity of markets declined. Shoppers were tempted by the all-year availability of imported produce, which ensured its constant supply, but meant that any sense of seasonality was lost.

Fortunately, a hankering for fresh, local produce, and for the pleasures of chatting to those who produce it, mean that farmers' markets have, for many of us, become part of the weekly shop. Each market is governed by strict rules and regulations, and all food comes from local farmers, growers, suppliers and producers within a small radius of the market; many are certified growers of organic produce. Since the first modern farmers' market opened in Bath in 1997, the numbers have risen to over 550 nationwide, and continue to grow as we spend our Saturdays filling bags with bundles of freshly pulled carrots and strings of free-range pork sausages.

Porthgain: The harbour village that built the roads of Britain

The popular perception of Wales is that it is a country of quarrying and mining. Pembrokeshire, however, is free of both and there is little evidence of industrial activities – until you get to Porthgain.

These days the village is busy with visitors eating in its fish restaurant, quaffing a pint in the Sloop Inn, or looking around its galleries and attractive harbour. One hundred years ago, however, the scene would have been very different. The large, sheltered harbour, tucked between the cliffs, was a powerhouse of Welsh industry fed by rich local reserves of granite and slate. Stone from the nearby quarries, linked to the harbour by tramways, was loaded onto ships for export. As the slate trade slackened, the village turned to brick making and stone crushing. Large hoppers, used to store granite prior to shipping, can still be seen here. For the best part of a century, the village echoed with the sound of crushers, saw mills and the noise of the brickworks which, at their peak, turned out up to 50,000 bricks a week.

What was once a little cove was extended into a substantial harbour so that bigger cargo ships could dock and load up with bricks and crushed granite. In the early 20th century, 4,000 tons of granite sailed out of Porthgain's harbour every month, destined to build roads all over Britain.

Below (left to right): Crab fishing pots in front of a brick wall; Porthgain Harbour.

Abereiddy and the Blue Lagoon

A tumbledown cottage, a ruined winch tower and a slate-grey beach are clues that this now lovely destination was once an industrial hub. Swimmers, divers and coasteerers usually head for the Blue Lagoon – a still, luminous pool that was once a quarry.

Abereiddy's quarry was deep and productive: slate was trundled away from here by horse-drawn tram to nearby Porthgain to be treated and then exported on cargo ships. When quarrying came to a halt, local fishermen blasted a hole in the sea wall to allow the sea to come in so that they could moor their boats in a safe environment.

What had been an industrial scar was transformed into a harbour and then, as fishing diminished, a destination for adrenaline junkies. Coasteering, a mix of swimming, climbing and jumping, began here in the 1990s and now attracts the reckless and the brave from around the globe, many of whom also come to watch and participate in the Cliff Diving World Series. Those in search of quieter pleasures also head here to walk the coastal path or enjoy a spot of wild swimming in the Blue Lagoon's eerie, shimmering water.

Above: The turquoise waters of the Blue Lagoon in Abereiddy.

THE COTSWOLDS

With its honey-coloured cottages and handsome churches, fields of corn and rolling hills, few regions epitomise English village life like the Cotswolds. Its picture-postcard villages tucked away down country lanes draw visitors by the coachload in the summer.

But what is the Cotswolds? It's not a county or a national park and the region has no official boundary. Its most celebrated area is a 800 sq. mile (2,072 sq. km) patch that extends across six counties, principally Gloucestershire and Oxfordshire, but also parts of Wiltshire, Somerset, Worcestershire and Warwickshire, sitting between the River Thames and the River Severn on a ridge of limestone that runs north-east from Somerset. This limestone has given the region two distinct characteristics: its distinctive golden stone and a grassland habitat ideal for sheep farming. In 1996 the Cotswolds was designated as an Area of Outstanding Natural Beauty (AONB) but it didn't need a designation to point out its loveliness. It is beautiful, and much of this is due to the appeal of its numerous, delightful villages.

Bibury: Quintessential Cotswolds

When thinking of a typical Cotswolds scene, the village of Bibury springs to mind. One of its streets, Arlington Row, a terrace of honey-coloured limestone cottages with steeply pitched roofs nestled beside the village green, is one of the most photographed in the UK (it has even appeared on the inside cover of the UK passport).

The Batsford guide described the village as follows: 'I might sum up the characters of Cotswold buildings in three swinging nouns. Solidity. Simplicity. And durability. The form is rectangular and its linear plains give them full effect, especially in rows of cottages as in Bibury.'

However, Arlington Row was not built to delight tourists and architectural historians – it was originally a monastic wool store, but was converted in the 17th century to house weavers and their families. They wove the wool in their cottages before taking it to Arlington Mill to be fauled – a process that involved dipping the wool in water and then stretching it. It is hard to imagine Bibury as such a hard-working place as it is now so upmarket and aspirational. The weavers' cottages are no longer a place for industrious textile production but smart and desirable residences.

Left: Arlington Row and Awkward Hill in the village of Bibury.
Right: The lovely honey-coloured cottages in Arlington Row.

Wool manufacturing has been vital to the Cotswolds and for centuries provided the main form of employment in the area. Central to all of this has been the Cotswold Lion, a breed of sheep with a lustrous, soft coat, which is thought to have been introduced by the Romans from North Africa. By the 12th century England was reputed to have the best wool in the world and the most desirable wool in England came from the Cotswolds. During the 16th century fortunes were made as mills were built to harness the power of the area's fast-flowing streams and turn the Cotswold Lion's fleece into textiles. Money from the wool industry built all the handsome churches and manor houses in the region but the decline of wool production in the area between 1750 and 1850 brought poverty and a fall in the number of Cotswold sheep. Fortunately, thanks to conservationists and rare-breed farmers the population is now growing once again. Look out for sheep with shaggy coats, a curly fringe, no horns, a white face, black nostrils and a fine dark line around the eyes.

Bisley: A sought-after village

The Cotswolds are often referred to as 'Notting Hill with Wellies', a reference to the number of folk who have moved here from London, or have second homes in the area. One of these is the author, dog lover and all-round good egg, Jilly Cooper. She moved to Bisley from Putney 30 years ago when she was writing her book *Riders*, which was set in the world of show jumping. She thought the Cotswolds would inspire her more than Putney Common. Jilly says that the villagers were very welcoming and looked after her when she first arrived. Some local people were terribly grand: 'You didn't ask any man what he did for a living,' says Jilly, 'he never did anything'. Grandest of all are members of the Royal Family: the Prince of Wales and the Duchess of Cornwall, Princess and Prince Michael of Kent and Princess Anne all live in adjacent villages.

Many TV personalities, actors, models and musicians, attracted by the beautiful homes and picturesque landscape, have also swapped their metropolitan existences for country life. David Beckham has been seen in the village and the actor Jamie Dornan who starred in *Fifty Shades of Grey* has also moved in. It looks like this once-rural community will keep its glamorous profile for a good while longer.

Slad and Laurie Lee

Many of our impressions of Cotswolds life have been formed by one book: *Cider With Rosie*. Its author, Laurie Lee, grew up in the village of Slad during the 1930s and his book is a paean to that time. It opens with one of his earliest memories, the day he got lost in the long grass: 'A tropic heat oozed up from the ground, rank with sharp odours of roots and nettles. High overhead ran frenzied larks, screaming as though the sky were tearing apart.' An alarming event for a young boy, but fortunately he was soon rescued by his sisters.

Laurie Lee sang in the church choir, attended school in the village and, when he was old enough, spent a great deal of time in The Woolpack, the village pub. Ironically, although his early life was thoroughly rural, he left the village when he was 19 to live in London, which was where he wrote the book. He came back when he had made his fortune, returning to the big city every so often, and is buried in the churchyard.

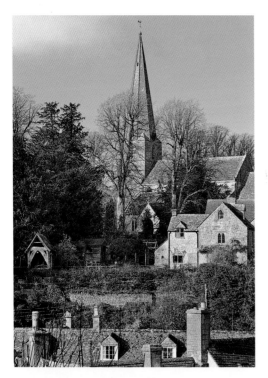

Above, top: The rooftops and church spire of Bisley.

Above: Laurie Lee, author of *Cider With Rosie*.

Left: Hazel Mill in Slad Valley.

Above: Evening sun over the Slad Valley.

Cider With Rosie is so evocative because it chronicles a lost era, a time when the world was changing and a faster pace of life was driving away things that had existed for thousands of years. As Lee writes:

'The change came late to our Cotswold valley ... my generation was born in a world of silence; a world of hard work and necessary patience, of backs bent to the ground, ... of white narrow roads, rutted by hooves and cartwheels, innocent of oil and petrol ... the horse was king.'

Blockley: Home of a remarkable woman and the British sidecar

As befits this area, Blockley has managed to make industry look very pretty indeed. The village, like others in the region, evolved around the production of wool. Back in the 1600s it was known as the village of water mills – its 12 wooden mills were strung out along the valley and powered by a single stream, Blockley Brook. But when the wool industry went into decline in the 18th century, the villagers nimbly found another way to create income and work: silk. Raw silk was imported from Asia to Coventry (35 miles/56.3km away) and then turned into fabric in Blockley. Blockley Brook's water has a high content of limestone that brought out the sheen of the silk.

The owner of Malvern Mill was a remarkable woman called Lucy Russell. When her husband died very young she was left in charge of the mill. Her workers 'threw' the silk, a process of washing, twisting and winding that became Blockley's speciality. Once the silk was thrown, it was bundled up and sent back to Coventry where it was woven into ribbons, an essential 19th century ball-gown accessory. During this time, over 3,000 people lived in Blockley and there were 70 shops – a small town by Victorian standards.

Lucy went on to run several mills but she left her village a more important legacy. There was a high incidence of cholera and typhoid in the village, sometimes as many as 70 cases a year. Lucy realised that the reason for this was that villagers drank directly from the brook that was shared with sheep and anything else that was discharged into it. She had five springs along the bank dammed and piped into a single outlet. Everyone was instructed to drink the pure water from the fountain and not from the brook. Cases of cholera and typhoid decreased immediately. Lucy's fountain can still be seen in the village by the road leadign to the mill: look out for the inscription, 'Water from the living rock. God's precious gift to man.'

By the 1800s, Britain was flooded with cheap silk products from abroad and the village adapted once more. One of the mills was converted to turn water power into electricity, bringing street lighting to Blockley when most towns and cities were still in the dark.

Above: Water mills can be spotted throughout the Cotswolds.

SIDECARS

In the days before a family car was the norm, the motorcycle was the vehicle of choice for many. In order to make them family-friendly, the addition of a sidecar was essential. These ultimate motorbike accessories have been made since 1912 by the Watsonian Motorcycle and Sidecar Company, which has its headquarters in Blockley. Although less common on the roads these days, sidecars have found a place on screen and have appeared in the *Harry Potter* films, while a Watsonian Jubilee sidecar transported Clarissa Dickson Wright around the country on the TV programme *Two Fat Ladies*.

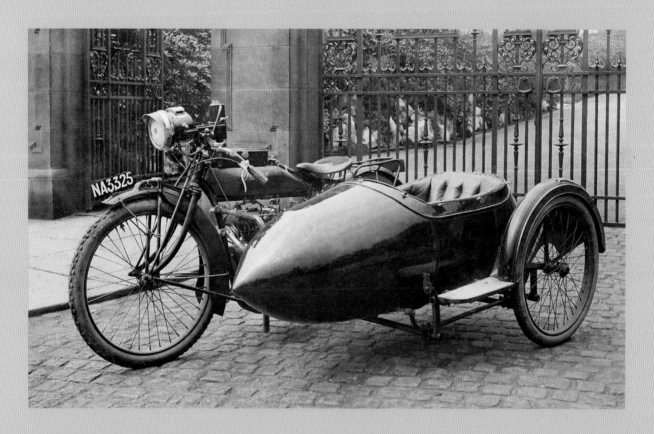

Hook Norton, an age-old industry and Aunt Sally

Cotswold villages now thrive on tourism and farming and few signs of industry remain apart from one exception: Hook Norton. The village has produced beer here for almost 170 years, ever since a farmer turned his hand to brewing in 1849 and founded Hook Norton Brewery. The beer is still delivered by horse-drawn dray – a cart pulled by two handsome shire horses, Nelson and Major.

Nelson and Major deliver beer to the local pub, the Pear Tree Inn, a couple of hundred yards down the lane from the brewery. This is just one of the traditions fostered by the landlord John Bellinger; another is a game called Aunt Sally. The game has been played in North Oxfordshire from at least the late 1800s and involves players throwing batons at a stubby white wooden skittle known as a doll. Aunt Sally was originally a figure of an old woman with a pipe in her mouth, but this has been modified for a more enlightened age. The game is played by two teams of eight players throwing six sticks per leg; it is played over three legs and the team that knocks down the highest number of dolls wins.

IT IS A FORTUNATE HEAD THAT NEVER ACHES.

Left: Working Shire horses from the brewery.

Right (top): A view of the Hook Norton Brewery.

Right (bottom): A greetings card from 1843 shows the game of Aunt Sally.

Alongside the post office and the church, the pub has always been the centre of the village. A sociable hub, traditionally it has been a place where villagers have gathered to chat, drink beer and meet friends and family. The pub with its genial landlord, not always genial regulars, phalanx of pumps and optics and the occasional dartboard, has long been a reassuring presence in British villages.

The origins of this British institution date back to when the Romans provided places for travellers to rest and find refreshment along their new roads. These watering holes continued to be used throughout the Middle Ages (the Tabard Inn is the hostelry that appears in Chaucer's *Canterbury Tales*) when they principally sold beer and ale. Gin, a cheap and potent alternative to beer, was introduced in the first half of the 18th century. The number of pubs peaked in the latter part of the 19th century when frequent incidents of drunkenness prompted Parliament to pass the Wine and Beerhouse Act in 1869 that tightened licensing rules.

Sadly, like the post office, the village pub is in danger. Cultural change (alcohol is now cheaper in supermarkets and rather than go out to drink, people prefer to drink at home), regulation and taxation have caused many to close. But all is not lost. Pubs have diversified, and the rise of the gastropub, pubs with rooms and child-friendly pubs, have given this most convivial meeting place a boost that, hopefully, will halt its further decline.

Common village pub names

Many village pub names are centuries old and provide clues to the life of the village in times past. Early names and signs) had to be simple and recognisable so that often-illiterate customers could understand them. Many originate from everyday, recognisable things:

Animal names
Dog and Duck, Fox and Hounds, Bull's Head

Heraldic origins
Bear and Ragged Staff, Red Lion, Elephant and Castle, Rising Sun

Livery companies
Three Arrows, Three Crowns, Three Horseshoes

Occupations
Bricklayer's Arms, Mason's Arms, Fisherman's Arms

Myths and legends
Black Horse, Green Man, The Silent Woman

Beer and wine
Barley Mow, Hop Pole, Three Tuns

Hunting and blood sports
Dog and Bear, Fox and Hounds, Tally Ho!

The Ampneys, Vaughan Williams and the Flying Nightingales

There are various Ampneys strung along Ampney Brook that flows into the Thames: Ampney St Mary Church, Ampney Crucis, Ampney St Peter and Down Ampney. It is the last Ampney that interests us here as it is the birthplace of that most English of composers, Ralph Vaughan Williams. When the nation was asked to choose its favourite Desert Island Disc in 2011, his composition 'Lark Ascending' topped the list. This violin and orchestra piece, inspired by a poem by George Meredith, conjures up visions of the English countryside like no other.

Vaughan Williams was born in 1872, the son of Down Ampney's vicar. Two years later the family moved to Surrey but Ralph never forgot the area. One of his operas *A Cotswold Romance* was about Cotswold life and his melody for the hymn 'Come Down, O Love Divine' was called 'Down Ampney'.

However, the serenity of Down Ampney that Vaughan Williams celebrated was shattered in late 1943. Across the fields from the church where he was baptised you can still see the remains of a military runway. This is RAF Down Ampney, one of three airfields that turned the Cotswolds into a transport hub during the Second World War. The Third Parachute Brigade set off from here on D-Day to be airdropped on Normandy, for example, and it was also the launching pad for an extraordinary, unsung group of women.

Although women made an enormous contribution during the war, generally they did not see active service. This was not true of the Flying Nightingales, a team of nursing orderlies who flew from Down Ampney on missions to evacuate casualties. A week after D-Day they flew to Normandy to care for injured soldiers and bring them back where necessary to be treated in buildings fully equipped as hospitals. Once assessed, the soldiers were taken on to more permanent facilities. In the first two months the 200 Flying Nightingales helped bring 20,000 wounded soldiers home. As the Allies pushed east across Belgium to the Rhine, those numbers increased and by the end of the war, almost 100,000 casualties had been returned to the Cotswolds.

Above: WAAF nursing orderlies standing in front of a Douglas Dakota Mark III.

Left: All Saints Church in Down Ampney.

Eighteen months after the war ended, the 2,500 servicemen and women left the base at Down Ampney, and it became a sleepy village once more. It was only in 2008 that Lifetime Service Awards were granted to the Flying Nightingales.

Ebrington and its village fête

Ebrington stands apart from other Cotswolds villages because of an unusual architectural element: some of its buildings are thatched. Apart from their distinctive roofs, the houses look familiar, built as they are from warm limestone. The iron oxide that occurs naturally in limestone is what makes the stone so honeyed, and the further north you travel, the darker the stone becomes.

The Batsford guide also draws attention to another unusual thing about Ebrington: the villagers' rivalry with a nearby village. The book explains that the people of Chipping Camden, 2 miles (3.2km) away, call the inhabitants of Ebrington Yabberton Yawnies – the implication being that they are boring. They also make fun of Ebrington's short church tower, comparing it with their own taller version and inventing a myth about it, which the guide also relates: the story goes that the villagers of Ebrington put muck on their tower to make it grow. An unlikely tale by all accounts, and as for the villagers being boring there's no sign of that at the annual village fête, which is a brilliant mix of fun and fundraising. The fête has been taking place on the cricket green one Saturday during the summer for over 40 years.

Left: Thatched roofing is unusual in the Cotswolds, but in Ebrington there are some fine exceptions.
Right: Summer roses climb across cottage doorways in Ebrington.

In summer, the verges of many country roads are lined with cheerful, handmade signs advertising the village fête. As the day (usually a Saturday in July) dawns, bunting is strung from trees, tables and tombola drums are hauled out of garages, and villagers approach the green with pots of jam or unwanted books and bric-a-brac. Behind the scenes, a committee has worked hard to ensure that a good variety of attractions is provided and a local celebrity has been secured to open proceedings. All that remains uncertain and unplanned is the weather.

'Fête' is a French word meaning 'holiday' or 'party', and the village fête is when the local community comes together to socialise and have fun. Originating in the 19th century, possibly growing out of larger, commercial fairs, village fêtes revolve around the agricultural calendar and are held when the crops are growing but the harvest is still a little way off. The village green is the obvious location but recreation grounds or the garden of the local manor house may also be put to good use. The village is spruced up, flowers are arranged in the church, and residents and visitors have a chance to behave foolishly, eat a lot of cake, buy pots of chutney that are never opened and shelter from the rain in the beer tent when the British weather is up to its usual tricks. In other words it is a thoroughly pleasant and charming way to spend a day.

Roll-up, roll-up: Village-fête attractions

The coconut shy: Wooden balls are thrown at a coconut perched on a pole. If the coconut is successfully dislodged, a prize may be claimed. (The word 'shy' means to toss or throw.) The origins of the game probably date back to the 19th century when coconuts were regarded as an exotic prize.

Tombola: Players draw a ticket from a revolving drum. If the number matches one taped to a prize, they could walk away with anything from a can of beans to a bottle of champagne.

White Elephant stall: A random selection of unwanted household bric-a-brac dug out of cupboards in the hope that a potential new owner may see its forgotten charms and buy it.

Home-made cakes: Local bakers get busy with their sponge tins to produce favourites including lemon drizzle, coffee and walnut, Victoria sponge and fruit scones.

Chutneys and jams: Fruit and veg gluts, which have been thriftily bottled and preserved, are sold to raise cash for village activities. Ever-inventive flavours (marrow and ginger, courgette and tomato, rhubarb and vanilla) tempt the taste buds of holidaymakers.

Dog show: Often a stand-alone event but frequently part of the village fête. Categories include the novelty – Prettiest Bitch, Waggiest Tail, Most Handsome Dog – alongside best of breeds. It is a chance for your pet to shine.

Bouncy castle: A modern introduction that allows parents to abandon children to tumble around on brightly coloured inflatable structures while they head for the beer tent.

rry up, children! Hi! Hi! Hi!
Who wants to have a cocoa-nut shy?"
y-boy misses, and so does May,
Ned knocks a cocoa-nut down – Hooray!
J-P

EAST ANGLIA

The ancient kingdom of East Anglia forms the well-known 'hump' on England's eastern side. It's a place of unspoiled rural landscape, vernacular architecture and long-held traditions. The Batsford guide to the region chose to visit just three counties: the flat, open lands of Suffolk, the coast and farming communities of Norfolk and the estuaries and meadows of Essex.

The landscape of East Anglia has inspired many artists, notably Thomas Gainsborough and John Constable, who were both born in Suffolk. Constable's pastoral depictions of his native county have become representative of its landscape: his painting *The Hay Wain*, which is based on a scene near Flatford on the River Stour, is emblematic of a lost rural past.

The region is still rooted in agriculture and is often referred to as the 'bread basket' of the nation: in Suffolk, about three-quarters of the land is farmed. But this does not mean that it is stuck in the past; in order to survive, its villages have had to adapt and have done this in a variety of nimble and enterprising ways.

Suffolk: Kersey, pretty as a picture

With medieval timber-framed cottages spilling down its hillside and a ford (known as 'the water splash') running through its centre, it's little wonder that Kersey has won accolades as one of East Anglia's prettiest villages. It made the cover of *The Batsford Guide to East Anglia*, painted by Brian Cook in pastel colours, and was described inside like this: 'The roofs of these old villages are as quaint as anything else about them. They are all of different heights and pitches and there is much variety of roofing material. The water splash gives delightful reflections. At the top of the hill at one end of the village the church stands like a crown just in the place where a church ought to stand. It is indeed a perfect village but it is becoming conscious of its beauty. One rarely passes through without seeing someone seated by the pavement doing a watercolour.'

Artists still put up their easels along the High Street and attempt to capture the idiosyncrasies of its Suffolk architecture. The village grew rich from the trade in cloth and wool during the Middle Ages (it was known for a coarse woollen cloth called Kersey cloth), which was when many of the weavers' cottages and merchants' houses were built. Houses were painted with limewash mixed with animals' blood to create a pink pigment – the older the animal the darker the colour – and constructed from wattle (wooden latticework) and daub (plaster made from chalk, clay, lime and dung), which was spread over it. The result is a mixture of pastel-coloured homes and black-and-white timber buildings, all of which provide endless subject matter for the watercolourists and sketchers who continue to pitch up to paint it.

Norfolk: Barton Turf and the Norfolk Broads

Norfolk has long been associated with the Broads, especially as a boating destination for holidaymakers, but what are they exactly? The Batsford guide gives us some clues, although not many helpful ones: 'It is the haunt of young men and maidens in sweaters and slacks. Two hundred miles [322km] of safe waterways lie ahead of the adventurers and even if they don't know much of seamanship, there's lots of chance to learn.

Above: A dog-walker strolling along the pretty streets of Kersey.

Left: A timber-framed pub in Kersey.

When one has described a couple of the reed-ringed lakes one has described them all. I can only add that this little patch of country is as different from anything else in England as chalk from cheese.'

The Broads are indeed a network of reed-ringed lakes, rivers and marshland. Created hundreds of years ago by the flooding of land depleted by medieval peat cutters, they stretch for over 117 sq. miles (303 sq. km), most of which is in Norfolk. Villages like Barton Turf sprung up along the water's edge to provide homes for peat cutters and for thatchers harvesting the reeds. The Broads have a total of 124 miles (200km) of navigable waterways and Barton Turf's history, like many villages in the area, is closely associated with the water and with boating. Britain's most famous sailor, Admiral Horatio Nelson, was Norfolk born and learned to sail here, and there has been a commercial boatyard in the village since 1883.

Left: A 1934 railway poster advertising the Norfolk Broads.

CAN YOU SPEAK NORFOLK?

It was once common for every region to have a traditional, local dialect but with the advent of TV, cars and general migration of people, they are dying out. Even back in the 1930s, the author of the Batsford guide was concerned that they were starting to disappear: 'Education and the BBC have done much to turn dialect speech into bastard cockney. I do not rejoice in it for the bastard cockney is an infinitely worse jargon than which it replaces. A man ought to speak either pure, unaffected and correct English or an honest-to-God dialect.'

Fortunately, a few dedicated organisations are keeping some dialects alive. One of these is the Friends of Norfolk Dialect. This poem, 'He couldn't get nuffin roight' is written by its chairman, Ted Peachman:

Old Ted he was a gardener/he loved his garden dear
But when them pests descended/cor blastboard did he swear.
The next year Ted got angry/he just set down and cried
He let that go to wilderness/And called that setticide.

Life on the water is still an important part of village life. Every August Bank Holiday, the Barton Broad Open Regatta brings competitors from nearby villages who moor on the Broad for the weekend. The regatta has been held since the 1800s when it was known as 'water frolics', although some of these 'frolics' involved offended professional helmsmen boarding other boats and becoming involved in punch-ups. Happily, things are much more genteel these days.

Norfolk: Flying high above the Snorings

The amusing names of the villages of Great and Little Snoring were not assigned because these are sleepy and peaceful places (although they are) but because of an Anglo Saxon derivation. 'Snare' refers to the settlement of that name and 'ingas' means a group of people; put them together and you have a settlement belonging to the people of Snare. Many names of British villages derive from Old English words and provide clues to their history (see page 128).

Today, the only disturbance in The Snorings might be a rumble of a tractor, but throughout the Second World War it was a different story. The airfield at Little Snoring was part of a network of airfields in East Anglia, each doing its part to defend Britain. By 1945 there were 37 military airfields in Norfolk. During the war, almost 2,000 service men and women were stationed in Little Snoring, and the skies above the county hummed with aircraft. Today only part of the old runway remains, but the village's aeronautical heritage is being kept alive by The Light Aircraft Company, which manufactures three different types of light aircraft – the Sherwood Ranger, the Sherwood Scout and the Sherwood Kub – and employs ten people. The village is now filled with the gentle sound of propellers turning as these elegant craft leave their hangars.

Above: Children play with the Miles Magist training plane at Little Snoring Primary School in 1952.

Right: The quaintly named village of Great Snoring.

Norfolk: Happisburgh's battles with the sea

Villagers are never more united than when fighting a common cause and the villagers in the Norfolk coastal village of Happisburgh have come together to take on a big adversary – the sea.

Happisburgh is a delightful place with a 15th-century church and thatched cottages built from flint and cobbles. However, its location, described as exhilarating in the Batsford guide in the 1930s, is now perilous: 'We meet beauty again at Happisburgh, pronounced "Hazeborough". It is set on a hill with cliffs and sea close below. The village is unspoiled and old though there are bungalows on the cliff edge a little distance off ... there is an exhilarating, perched-up feeling about Happisburgh; the sea is far below, and the country inland falls away, too, giving enormous views.'

Coastal erosion is eating away at the cliff at the alarming rate of 16½–33ft (5–10m) a year. The villagers had spent years seeking compensation for damage caused by rising sea levels and campaigning for better sea defences to be constructed, so when the devastating storms of 2003 hit, they had had enough. Hundreds of people gathered on the cliffs and formed themselves into three gigantic letters: SOS ('Save Our Shoreline'). The protest was the start of a campaign that prompted the government to set up a £10 million fund to help flood-endangered and hard-hit coastal communities. The village might not be able to hold back the sea but they now have the resources to minimise its damage.

This stretch of Norfolk coast isn't just treacherous for homeowners – storms have also claimed the lives of numerous seafarers, too. In 1801, Admiral Nelson was waiting for HMS *Invincible* to join his fleet bound for the Battle of Copenhagen. It never appeared. Instead it foundered off Happisburgh; 400 of the crew of 590 were lost and are buried in the village churchyard.

In modern times, anyone in difficulty in the sea will depend on the plucky members of the local RNLI crew. Receiving 11 call-outs (or 'shouts') and around

Above: A horse grazes in front of Happisburgh Lighthouse.

20 safety interventions a year, the volunteers need to be in a permanent state of readiness. There has been a lifeboat station on the cliffs here since 1866 but during the storms of 2002, the lifeboat station itself fell victim to coastal erosion and the ramp was swept into the sea. Fortunately, a new building further down the coast now provides a bigger ramp, better facilities and some new recruits.

Above: The eroded coastline at Happisburgh.

Suffolk: The horticultural association that saved Newbourne

A village's survival is often down to its ability to embrace change. During the 1930s, the village of Newbourne had a dwindling population and an unpromising future. In order to survive it underwent a radical transformation. The Land Settlement Association took families from deprived areas of high unemployment in industrial Britain and placed them in rural communities with dwindling populations. Newbourne was one such place.

Long-term unemployed from the North East, many of whom had been fishermen or boat builders, moved to Newbourne to become smallholders. The village tripled in size as around 50 Tyneside workers and their families moved south to learn about horticulture and develop their own businesses. Each family received three months' training, a house, a piggery or cattle, a glasshouse and 5–10 acres (2–4ha) of land. The scheme ended with the start of the Second World War and the settlements were dissolved and privatised in 1983.

Most of the glasshouses, once brimming with vegetables ready for market, have now fallen into disrepair but a new wave of incomers have taken some of them on. Plant nurseries and roadside produce stalls serve as a reminder of the bold initiative that made smallholders out of shipbuilders.

Right: The Church of St Mary in Newbourne.
Far right: Wisteria grows across a doorway in Newbourne.

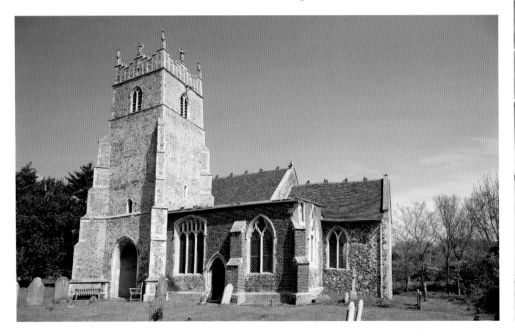

Essex: Silver End and a kindly benefactor

For generations, the prosperity and welfare of village communities relied on the patronage and generosity of others, whether it was the local aristocratic family or a rich landowner. In more recent times this philanthropy took a new direction as industrialists built villages and towns with the well-being of their workers in mind.

Silver End is one such place and it grew from one man's vision. In 1926 Francis Henry Crittall, who had made his fortune manufacturing metal windows, built a new village for his workforce. Crittall windows had achieved

Below: A flat-roofed house with Crittall windows in Silver End.

great success, and had been installed around the world, as well as in the Houses of Parliament and the Tower of London. Crittall, who was known as 'The Guv'nor', employed architect Thomas S. Tait, a proponent of the Art Deco style, to design the buildings for his garden village. The result was homes that now, although in some disrepair, are splendid examples of modernist architecture. Every house had hot and cold running water, and front and rear gardens. Silver End boasted a large department store, a hotel, and an enormous village hall with a dance floor, cinema, library and clinic. Crittall, it seemed, had thought of everything.

The Guv'nor lived in Silver End himself and kept a kindly but watchful eye over his workforce. His aim was to nurture a happy, healthy – and therefore productive – workforce. It seems to have paid off: business boomed and Crittall was well thought of by his grateful employees many of whom worked for the company their entire lives. After his death, they made some gates and lamps in his memory. The inscription on the gates reads: 'These gates and lamps were made by the voluntary labour of the firm's employees past and present in the grateful memory of The Guv'nor and his wife.'

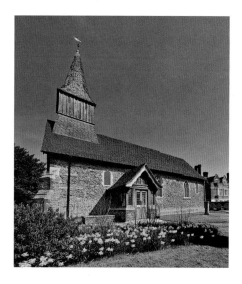

Essex: Woodham Walter and Bell Meadow Day

A more recent act of philanthropy changed the face of Essex village Woodham Walter. Four generations of the Durham family have lived here since 1904, managing an apple farm of about 100 acres (40.5ha). When a patch of land called Bell Meadow was in danger of being redeveloped, John Durham and his family stepped in, and secured a deal with Essex and Suffolk Water that gifted Bell Meadow to the village.

Since 2005 over the August Bank Holiday, the people of Woodham Walter remember this generous gift on Bell Meadow Day, with a village country fair. The Durham family were invited to cut the tape to open the first fair officially and the event has become bigger every year since then. Alongside food stalls and country crafts, activities include dog beauty contests, an egg-throwing competition and demonstrations by local bee-keepers and ice-hockey players. It is the perfect opportunity for the village to come together and have fun, and this sense of community is what is keeping it, and other villages, alive and flourishing.

Above: St Margaret's Parish Church, Woodham Mortimer.

You can tell a lot about a village by its name. Most are inspired by the people who settled there, the wildlife, or the landscape around them, and contain, for example, Old English, Welsh, Old Norse or Cumbric terms that relate to them. Here are a few examples:

'blen' (Cumbric, Welsh): fell, hill, upland, e.g. Blencathra

'borne' (Old English): brook, e.g. Sittingbourne

'by' (Old Norse): village, e.g. Derby, Formby, Rugby

'chipping' (Old English): market, e.g. Chipping Camden

'coed' (Welsh): wood, forest, e.g. Betws-y-coed

'cwm' (Welsh): valley, e.g. Cwmbran

'den' (Old English): valley, e.g. Todmorden

'ham' (Old English): farm or homestead, e.g. Chippenham

'lan', lhan, llan' (Welsh): church e.g. Llanelli

'mere' (Old English): lake, pool, e.g. Grasmere

'pen' (Cumbric, Welsh, Cornish): headland, e.g. Pendle, Penzance

'shep' (Old English): sheep, e.g. Shepton Mallet

'stow' (Old English): place of assembly, e.g. Stow-on-the-Wold

'weald' or 'wold' (Old English): high woodland, e.g. Southwold

BRIAN COOK

THE SOUTH WEST

The counties of Dorset, Somerset and Wiltshire all formed part of the Anglo-Saxon region known as Wessex. Although the term subsequently fell out of use, it was kept alive by Thomas Hardy who portrayed its rural life so vividly in his books.

Hardy, the son of a stonemason, was born in Higher Bockhampton, a hamlet near Dorchester in Dorset, in 1840. He drew on the landscape and the lives of the people around him for his poetry and novels set in his romanticised county of Wessex. Hardy's books, which include *Far From the Madding Crowd*, *Tess of the d'Urbervilles* and *Jude the Obscure*, recount not just the beauty of the landscape but the hard, often violent, lives of the people who inhabited it. His characters' struggles with their social standing, misunderstandings and their inescapable fate, describe a realistic village existence that is a counterpoint to many idealised views of country life.

Many of the villages are ancient and unspoiled, and give a flavour of what life was like in Hardy's time.

Somerset: Montacute

Despite its fine medieval church and picturesque cottages, Montacute did not find favour with the author of the Batsford guide: 'It is a fine village, as one might say a fine woman with a touch of brazenness in the way it displays itself, and with little of the seductive charm of some villages.' Perhaps he was having a bad day or thought that the other villages nearby outshone its charms.

Whatever the reason, today we can appreciate its limestone buildings, many of which were built by the Phelips family of Montacute House as part of their estate. Montacute House, an impressive, late-Elizabethan house and garden, is owned and managed by the National Trust. Completed in 1601, it was the home of Sir Edward Phelips who created this mansion of glass and a type of limestone known as ham stone, as a representation of his wealth and status. Over the border in Wiltshire is another National Trust property with a different story to tell.

Below: Montacute House, now owned by the National Trust.

Wiltshire: Lacock and William Henry Fox Talbot

It's unsurprising that the village of Lacock, with its half-timbered houses jostling amongst stone cottages and a medieval tithe barn, has been used countless times as a film location. Most of the village is owned by the National Trust and it is largely unaffected by the coming of modernity. *Pride and Prejudice*, *Moll Flanders*, *Emma* and some of *Harry Potter* have all been filmed here.

At the heart of the village is Lacock Abbey, an eccentric building of various architectural styles that was built on the foundations of a former nunnery. It was also the home of a pioneer of photography – William Henry Fox Talbot – whose achievements are celebrated in a museum inside.

In 1834, Fox Talbot invented the negative/positive photographic process, which enabled us to see and record the world in a completely different way. Disappointed by his lack of ability as an artist (he described his drawings as 'melancholy to behold'), he decided to create a machine that could do the drawing for him. His first forays into photography took place at Lacock when he photographed a window through a rough little wooden box fitted with a lens. He went on to record scenes in his neighbourhood, including Lacock village, which are a remarkable record of rural life over 150 years ago.

Wiltshire: Castle Combe, too good to be true?

It's a hard accolade to live up to, but Castle Combe, named 'Prettiest Village in England' by the British Travel Association in the early 1960s, is managing to do it. Its loveliness was recognised a decade earlier in the Batsford guide to the region: 'At first sight it seems almost too good to be true with its golden stone and

Above (top): Henry Fox Talbot at his makeshift studio.

Above (bottom): An ivy-clad cottage in Lacock.

ochre or salmon-coloured houses lining the twisting lanes. There is a picturesque village shop or two, a comfortable-looking inn and a market cross all protected by roofs of stout grey stone slates, above which rises the tall 15th-century tower of the church, backed by steep hangers of beech woods. It seems indeed like the ideal English village produced for a film set rather than the genuine article.'

The centuries-old houses that line the road as it winds its way down towards the river don't just look like a film set, they have been used as such many times. The most notable of these was *Doctor Dolittle*, which was filmed here in 1966, causing some residents, angry at modifications made to the area, to sabotage filming. More recently, Steven Spielberg shot *War Horse* in the village, and it was also the location for an episode of *Downton Abbey*.

It's not all rural idyll in Castle Combe, however. Just outside the village on a former airfield, is a highly challenging 20 mile (32 km) motor-racing track; one of its bends, Quarry Corner, is regarded as the most technically difficult in British motorsport.

Castle Combe Circuit was the brainchild of Kay Thomas, a local landowner and motor-racing enthusiast, who created the circuit with a local car club in 1950. During its first decade Castle Combe attracted all the big names on the motor-racing circuit, including Stirling Moss, Mike Hawthorn and John Surtees. It continues to draw big names and large crowds and has featured on the TV programme *Top Gear*. Jeremy Clarkson described the circuit as 'a fierce track, one of the fastest in Britain'.

Above: Classic car racing at Castle Combe Circuit.
Left: The picturesque village of Castle Combe.

Wiltshire: When is a village a town? When it's Mere

The view of Mere on the cover of the Batsford book *English Village Homes* has barely changed since Brian Cook painted it in the 1930s. The trees have grown of course but the church and houses are the same. The only problem is that although Mere feels like a village, with its rows of cottages and church spire, it is actually a town. Which begs the question: what is the definition of a village?

The answer is not clear-cut. Most agree that a village must have a church, a market place, a village hall or community centre, a village green, a pub, houses and shops, but there are no hard and fast rules. Mere, for example, may look like a village now but its history has been as a town. During the 14th century it was a prosperous place, grown rich on wool money, with a market house, guildhall and wide streets, and a position on the main London to Exeter road. But by the 18th century, with road improvements and turnpiking, the nearby settlements of Shaftesbury, Frome, Bruton and Sherborne were on the rise, and Mere's importance started to wane.

Our perceptions of what a village should look like are relatively new. Beginning in the Middle Ages it was advantageous for any settlement to have some kind of town or market charter. With that in place, fortunes would massively improve. From the late 19th century onwards, however, the romantic notion of the village as a quiet retreat – somewhere to escape the noise of towns and cities – began to grow. Town status became less important as the concept of a rural idyll captured our imaginations.

Dorset: The thatched village of Chideock

One feature that is so evocative of the British village is the thatched roof. Although thatch can be found throughout the country, Dorset boasts an impressive 12 per cent of the total, and the village of Chideock is home to 72 properties with thatched roofs – all of which have been thatched by one man,

Above: A view of village square from the Clock Tower at Mere.

Dave Symonds. Dave has been thatching for 50 years, starting in the trade straight from school at the age of 15. He has been in constant employment ever since; there is plenty to occupy him – thatched roofs need attention every ten years, and a re-thatch every 20 or 25.

Dave is carrying on a traditional craft that can be traced back to the Bronze Age. The tools he uses have hardly changed for hundreds of years. His legget, the tool used to give the reeds an even finish, is the very one he used as an apprentice. There are subtle regional variations in thatching styles, the Dorset style is said to resemble poured custard, and conservation regulations dictate that the thatch must be made from wheat straw. As this can be hard to get hold of Dave grows his own – a traditional variety with longer stalks. The wheat is threshed to remove the ears before it is bundled ready for thatching.

Dave is not just the village thatcher, he is also a bell ringer at the church. The bells have rung out in Chideock for over 400 years but, when the bell frame became unstable in 2011, they almost fell silent. This was inconceivable to Dave and the local community so they got together and raised £70,000 in just nine months to save them. The bells, rung by the villagers, will continue to chime for generations to come.

Above: A thatched cottage at Chideock.

Whether it's to call the faithful to prayer, a merry peal at a wedding or a solemn single bell tolling as a mark of a respect, church bells often provide the soundtrack to village life.

Bell-ringing in churches can be traced back to the 8th century but it was only in the 1600s that tuned bells started to be rung in patterns called 'changes' (which is the origin of phrase 'ringing the changes'). Bells in church towers are hung so that on each stroke, the bell swings through a complete circle. Between strokes, it briefly sits upside down with its mouth pointing upwards. A rope connected to a large wheel is pulled to swing it down, and then the mechanism pulls it back up again. Each alternate pull or stroke is either a handstroke or backstroke. Six or eight bells are common, but some churches have up to 16, and each bell needs a ringer.

DING DONG MERRILY: INTERESTING BELL-RINGING FACTS

- During the Middle Ages, popular superstition had it that bells could ring themselves. It was said that those at Canterbury Cathedral tolled themselves when Thomas à Becket was murdered in 1170.
- In rural areas during the 18th century, bell-ringers' standards of behaviour deteriorated, and many were described as layabouts and drunks.
- Miss Alice White of Basingstoke was the first woman to take up bell-ringing in 1896. The Ladies Guild of Change Ringers was formed in 1912.
- Bells were silenced during the Second World War with the instruction that they were to ring only to inform of an enemy invasion. When peace was declared in 1945 the bells rang one more.
- The largest national bell-ringing event took place to mark the Millennium – approximately 95 per cent of all church bells in the UK were rung on 1 January 2000.

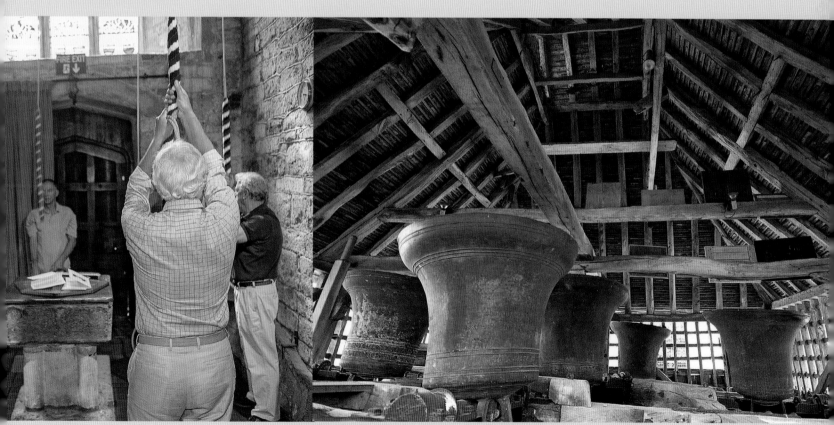

Dorset: Poundbury, a very modern village

Appearances can be deceptive at Poundbury. At first glance, its variety of architectural styles, from Georgian to Classical to vernacular, suggests that it has been around for centuries. But a second view reveals that the buildings are unblemished, made from modern materials and part of a grander scheme.

Poundbury was only started in 1993, on land owned by the Duchy of Cornwall. It is the manifestation of the Prince of Wales' architectural vision, and follows the principles of urban and rural planning set out in his book, *A Vision of Britain: A Personal View of Architecture*. His idea was to take the blueprint of a successful village and apply it to a modern settlement. The result is a community where shops and businesses are integrated with private and social housing. Any evidence of utilities is hidden in ducts or disguised as architectural features, and sustainable development informs all building and planning decisions. The current inhabitants are encouraged to practice neighbourliness and foster a sense of community, and there is a book of rules called *Living in Poundbury* to guide them along the right path.

Its opening paragraph reads: 'We hope this will be helpful to you and provide some answers to common problems. In essence, the success of the community in Poundbury depends on courtesy to others, good neighbourliness and talking to your neighbours and compliance with the covenants and stipulations.'

The book states that residents require consent from the Duchy to paint or decorate the exterior of their houses. No caravans or boats are allowed on their property and as loose gravel around public areas is causing a problem with cat mess, they are encouraged to offer alternatives.

The rules don't seem to have put anyone off living in Poundbury; the village continues to expand and by 2025 the number of homes is likely to have increased to 6,000.

Above and left: The various architectural styles at Poundbury.

Dorset: Fishing at West Bay

Many coastal villages around the UK developed as a result of fishing. The livelihoods of the villagers were dependent on what could be caught at sea, and fishing defined the life and activities of the community. These days, fishermen's cottages and harbours pull in more tourists than daily catches. In the 1930s, there were 47,000 fishermen in Britain, now there are less than 13,000, and the average catch then was 14 times what it is now.

Even back in the 1930s, when the Batsford guide was written, West Bay near Bridport, once a busy fishing village, was flagging: 'It is perhaps a slight exaggeration to call West Bay a port, for it is in no sense a refuge for shipping since the little harbour formed by stone and wooden piers is only accessible in fair weather. If as a harbour it is dwindling in importance, as a pleasure resort it is growing.'

Although it is a tough way to earn a living, fishing is still a vital business for smaller coastal communities who have had to evolve to survive. These days the catch is lobster and crab rather than the dwindling numbers of wet fish regulated by quotas. Most of the crab is sold to Spain and France but there is a big market for lobster in the UK. All of them are measured carefully to ensure

Left: Fishing nets piled over a wall.

Below, left: Houses on the beach front at West Bay.

Below: The ordered thatched cottages at Milton Abbas.

that the young ones aren't taken too early. There is some anxiety that even this method of fishing will dwindle as set-up costs and the high license fee may prohibit the younger generation from taking it up. If that does happen, West Bay and other fishing communities like it, will lose a little bit of their heart and soul.

Dorset: Milton Abbas, an 18th-century village in the modern world

Milton Abbas is just as beautiful today as it was when the Batsford guide was written in the 1950s: 'Blocks of semi-detached cottages of identical design are spaced along either side of the wide road and a chestnut tree planted between each block. The result is a village whose equal in serenity and quiet charm it would be hard to find. Nature and artifice are in complete harmony. The street bends with the turn of the valley, the banked-up woods are to be seen at hand and the spreading chestnut trees bring nature into the street.'

The village certainly looks orderly with its 36 identical thatched cottages spaced at regular intervals on either side of a curving street – a clue that the settlement did not grow organically. In fact, it was built in 1780 according to the whim of local landowner and owner of Milton Abbey, Lord Milton, who found the adjacent market town of Middleton not to his liking and spoiling his view. As a consequence, Middleton was demolished, Lord Milton commissioned architect Sir William Chambers and landscape designer Capability Brown to build a new village, and the Middleton inhabitants were moved in.

However, what suited the villagers in the 18th century, doesn't always suit modern family life. The semi-detached cottages are small and conservation rules prevent any alterations or extensions. Residents tend to move on as their families grow and more space is needed.

A fluid population is one of the greatest challenges that modern villages face. In previous generations, residents tended to work where they lived, bringing prosperity and stability. With rocketing house prices and the profusion of second homes, this is becoming increasingly rare. Farmers, for example, may farm the land around the village but, driven out by property prices, live elsewhere and have to commute to work. The danger is that villages become dormitories for city commuters or fill up with holiday homes as the original community is pushed out.

Somerset: Muchelney, surfacing from the floods

The village way of life is not just threatened by economics; the natural world can also be a menace, specifically the dangers of flooding. Nowhere is this more evident than the Somerset Levels where the village of Muchelney was cut off for ten weeks during the floods in the winter of 2013. Water levels rose to 14in (35.6cm) in some houses, causing damage that has taken a long time to repair. Increasingly isolated, the community felt abandoned and forgotten, until the Prince of Wales paid a visit and the media picked up the story. It wasn't this attention that made the real difference, however, it was the community pulling together. The villagers tried their best to carry on as normal – the vicar arrived on a boat every Sunday to hold a service in the church, and villagers supported one another over broken toes or the loss of a pet.

After the flood, a £20 million fund was put in place to restore property and to clear the watercourses. There has been much discussion about how to minimise future flood damage. Some blame the lack of land management and failure to drain ditches and waterways to cope with the high level of water. Others say house building on flood plains caused water to run off rather than

Left: A pontoon bridge across the flood water at Mulchelney.

Below: Riding is one of the more traditional diversions open to the village youth.

drain into the ground. Since 2013 the floods have not returned but the anxiety that they might is always present in Muchelney.

Wiltshire: The enterprising youth of Aldbourne

Much is said on the subject of villages losing post offices, shops and pubs, and how this contributes to young people drifting away from where they grew up. However, things are different in Aldbourne: there is a florist, a hairdresser, a supermarket, a post office and, most interestingly, there is the headquarters of Aldbourne Village Youth Council.

This enterprising, award-winning project began when a group of young people decided to do something about the lack of facilities in the village. They started by raising funds to build a BMX track on a piece of vacant land, and once that was achieved went on to organise a variety of community projects, from making and selling chocolate to helping with a charity shop, internet café and holiday cottage. All the money they raise goes back into the Youth Council to help fund their next enterprising initiative.

This spirit of enterprise surfaces elsewhere in the village, this time in a more traditional business: the smithy. The furnace in the smithy went out in the 1980s when blacksmith Alan Liddiard died from a brain tumour. It remained unlit for 30 years until his great nephew, Marc Hart, decided to give up his job as an accountant and return to the forge. He reopened the smithy and found all the tools and the anvil undisturbed and ready for business. Now the business is in its fifth year and flourishing – a traditional skill now has a new lease of life.

Above: A 1797 card depicting a wife selling at market.

Somerset: A long history of merry making and wife selling at Yarlington

The village fête, that most notable day of the year, is sometimes held in the grounds of the local manor house. There has been a summer fair at Yarlington for 700 years and these days it is held in Yarlington House, home of Carolyn, Countess de Salis. Back in the Middle Ages, fairs were often rowdy events and the scene of riots, so you had to have a charter to hold one: Simon de Montacute obtained one for Yarlington in 1314.

An unpleasant episode occurred at the fair in 1789 when Mr Atweel was recorded as selling his wife to Mr Wadman for five shillings, and she was led away with a halter around her neck. Although wife selling wasn't common it certainly did occur: between 1780 and 1850, 300 cases were reported. As divorce was off limits to the poor, it was the only way to end an unsatisfactory marriage. Thomas Hardy supposedly used the Yarlington incident as the basis for the plot for *The Mayor of Casterbridge* – Michael Henchard gets drunk and auctions his wife and baby daughter to a sailor for five guineas.

Happily there are no such activities at Yarlington Fayre these days: a dog show, archery range and a brass band are more than sufficient to keep visitors fully entertained.

The smithy's forge was once commonplace in British villages. It was the place everyone went to have anything metal made or repaired. The blacksmith, standing beside his blazing furnace, his hammer clanging against the anvil, was as central to village life as the vicar or postman. He would create objects by heating wrought iron or steel until the metal became soft enough to shape. This required a great deal of strength, as the poem 'The Village Blacksmith' by Henry Wadsworth Longfellow describes:

> Under a spreading chestnut-tree
> The village smithy stands;
> The smith, a mighty man is he,
> With large and sinewy hands;

> And the muscles of his brawny arms
> Are strong as iron bands.'
> ...
> Week in, week out, from morn till night,
> You can hear his bellow blow;
> You can hear him swing his heavy sledge,
> With measured beat and slow,
> Like a sexton ringing the village bell,
> When the evening sun is low.

A renewed interest in rural crafts has led to a revival in blacksmithing, although these days a blacksmith is more likely to create a piece of decorative ironwork for the garden or an ornamental gate, than he is fix the crankshaft of a tractor.

SUSSEX AND KENT

The villages of Sussex and Kent are as varied as the landscape. The chalk downland of the South Downs (the UK's newest national park) rolls towards the sea and is dotted with flint cottages and half-timbered houses; the High Weald that stretches from Surrey in the east to the Kent coast in the west has grand homes and country gardens; the Kent countryside is peppered with oast houses, while its coast boasts weatherboard cottages and handsome bungalows.

Whatever the style of the buildings, each village has its own story to tell, whether it's the making of a cricket bat, the generosity of a landowner, or the legend of conjoined twins. The Batsford guides went in search of village landmarks, and these two counties provided plenty of examples, from elaborate village signs to war memorials and grand follies.

These symbols represent insights into our history and traditions, often displaying that most English of characteristics: eccentricity.

Sussex

The Independent State of Cuckfield

For many years, the village of Cuckfield was known as the Ascot of the donkey world. Up to 10,000 people attended its annual Donkey Grand National for a lively and unusual day at the races. Donkey jockeys came from local pony clubs, 20 bookmakers set up their stalls, and all the money raised went to local charitable causes. Unfortunately, in 1965, the playing fields in which the races were held were compulsorily purchased by the local council and no more donkey races were allowed. Not only did this mean an end to a most enjoyable event but no more money was raised for the village.

Rather than concede defeat, the enterprising villagers dreamt up an alternative money-raising scheme. They declared independence for Cuckfield, a tongue-in-cheek title with a charitable hook: votes for the mayor could be bought for one penny each, with the winner being the candidate that received the most votes. The position of mayor is purely honorary and all the ill-gotten gains of from this splendidly corrupt electoral system supports local charities. The current mayor is the pub landlord, Rob Helliwell, who swept to power on votes costing £4,200 – all of which went to 30 different organisations. Vivat Cuckfield! Long may it prosper.

Alfriston, quintessentially Sussex

Further along the Cuckmere Valley sits the picturesque village of Alfriston. The village's half-timbered buildings, flint cottages, village green and ancient church nestled at the foot of the South Downs led the writer of the Batsford guide to describe it as 'one of Sussex's professional beauties'. This loveliness is believed to have inspired Eleanor Farjeon to write the words to that joyful hymn 'Morning Has Broken' in 1931, which was released as a single by Cat Stevens in 1972.

Flint runs through the chalk of the South Downs and often appears along footpaths. Unlike the porous chalk that surrounds it, it is a hard material, closely related to quartz, which when split can be shaped or 'knapped' to create a smooth, sharp surface; ideal, then, for use as a building material. Knapped flint and flint cobbles are seen in the walls of many houses all over Sussex,

Above: A 1790 card showing the Cuckfield village fair.

Right: A misty morning across the Cuckmere Valley.

VERNACULAR VILLAGE ARCHITECTURE

The oldest buildings in any village, and those that give it its character, weren't designed by professional architects. Stone cottages, medieval barns and black-and-white timber houses were built following the traditions of the area using the skills of the local builders. These 'vernacular' buildings reflect the culture and history of the village, with styles varying across the country.

Stone cottages vary depending on what stone was available, and the wealth of the home owner. Poorer cottages generally had thicker walls, built with roughly shaped stones – what is known as 'rubble masonry'. They have solid quoins (cornerstones) to give the wall stability and were frequently finished with lime mortar to give a smoother finish and help rain run off.

If more money was available, houses were built from stone cut to a higher standard and with smooth surfaces and joints – what is known as 'ashlar masonry'. Stone lintels were also added on windows and doors. Ashlar buildings were limewashed to protect the stone. (Many stone cottages have lost their original mortar or limewash finish and are effectively naked.)

Timber-framed buildings: if no stone was available, houses were built from timber, usually immediately after it was felled when it was still 'green' and unseasoned. A large medieval farmhouse could use up to 300 oak trees, whereas a one-room cottage could be made from two small trees. These buildings rarely

had foundations, and were built on top of stone pads. There are two main types of timber-framed buildings.

- Cruck-frame buildings are constructed from large timbers made from the same bough of a tree to create an A-frame at each end of the building, and sometimes along its length. Horizontal tie beams and diagonal braces ran between the crucks to make it secure. Initially cruck frames were only used on high-status medieval buildings, but from the late 1500s poorer, single-storey properties and barns were also built using a cruck frame.
- Box frames and post-and-truss frames are made of large vertical and horizontal timbers fixed together in a cube shape. This is the typical construction of many Tudor buildings, where often the upper storey would overhang the lower one.

  Both styles of timber-framed buildings used wattle and daub: panels of woven timber (wattle) coated and filled with a mixture of dung, clay and chopped straw (daub), sealed with limewash.

Cob cottages made from compacted earth are found where stone or timber is not in plentiful supply. Cob is a mix of horsehair, straw or dung, thrown down in layers and creates thick walls (up to 4ft/1.2m), which are gently rounded.

including several in Alfriston, such the Clergy House (the first building acquired by the National Trust in 1896), which was built in the 14th century, and it is a style of architecture that has become synonymous with the county.

Below: The village of Telscombe nestled within the South Downs.

Telscombe, a village preserved

No public road leads to Telscombe. Although the village is nearly 2 miles (3km) from the coast, it is reached by driving down a single, dead-end track off the busy Lewes to Newhaven road. Its cluster of buildings, including a 10th-century church, feels untouched and forgotten. The enduring charm and detachment of

this village is the legacy of one man: Ambrose Gorham. A successful bookmaker and racehorse trainer, Gorham moved to Telscombe in the late 1800s because the downland of Telscombe Tye provided the ideal conditions to keep his racing stock in good shape.

In 1902 he hit the big time when one of his horses, *Shannon Lass*, won the Grand National. Gorham channelled his wealth and energy into this poor and tiny rural community. He brought electricity and water to Telscombe (previously everyone had drunk rainwater from their roofs), refurbished the church and other village buildings, and built a brand new village hall.

Gorham was also a keen amateur photographer and, in 1904, set out to record the life of the village. Looking at the pictures now, apart from the clothes of the villagers, little has changed. This is also down to Gorham. When he died in 1933, he left his many properties and acres of land to be managed by a trust that preserves and cares for it. Whereas nearby stretches of the coast have been gobbled up by property developers, Telscombe remains just as it has always been: a little pocket of undisturbed rural life.

West Hoathly and the first cultivated cottage garden

The village of West Hoathly is one of a scattering of villages that sit high on a ridge on the High Weald. 'Weald' is the Old English word for woodland – a clue to the fact that at one time the valleys and hills surrounding it were forested. Settlements were built on the higher, less boggy land and West Hoathly, with its church, pub and priest's house, is typical of the area. What is less typical, however, is the country garden of the manor house, Gravetye Manor.

The gardens at Gravetye were the creation of an Irishman, William Robinson, who rose through Victorian society to become one of the most respected horticulturalists of his time. Robinson outlined his philosophy in his book, *The Wild Garden*, in which he rejected the straitjacket of conventional planting schemes in favour of greater informality. He had no time for topiary (which he called 'cruelty to hedges'), planted-out bedding schemes, statuary or standard roses. Instead, he cultivated a natural style of gardening with mixed herbaceous borders and dense planting of hardy perennials and native plants, which became the foundation of the style we call 'cottage gardening'.

When his writing career led to financial success, he bought Gravetye Manor and its 200 acres (81ha) of land, which provided the opportunity to put his new ideas into practice. He put 50 years of love and hard work in the garden,

Left: Gravetye Manor seen from across the flower garden.

Below: Rudyard Kipling's study at Bateman's, his home in Burwash.

including the planting of hundreds of trees, before he died aged 96 in 1935. Gravetye Manor is now a luxury hotel and the garden is cared for by head gardener Tom Coward who is doing much to restore and preserve its influential heritage.

Burwash, home of Rudyard Kipling

Further east in the Weald is the village of Burwash, most notable for being the home of author Rudyard Kipling who lived here for half of his life. These days we remember Kipling for titles such as *The Jungle Book* and *Puck of Pook's Hill*, but in Burwash there is a reminder of his contribution to village life: the war memorial.

In August 1914, Kipling had been instrumental in arranging for his 17-year-old son John (also known as Jack) to enrol in the army. Thirteen months later, at the Battle of Loos, John was killed. In the war's aftermath, his father channelled his grief into becoming an active member of the War Graves Commission. Kipling chose some of our most memorable war engravings,

Although war memorials first appeared in the UK following the Boer War (1899–1902), numbers rose significantly after the First World War when 700,000 soldiers lost their lives, and again after the Second World War. The need for a place to focus national grief and to remember those who had died led to villages erecting monuments in public places. Memorials varied in style from sculpted figures to crosses and obelisks, but most featured a roll call of names of the local people who had been killed in conflict. It is estimated that there are 100,000 war memorials in the UK; they are an important part of our cultural and military heritage and a gathering place to honour the dead on Remembrance Day.

159

including 'Their names liveth forever more' and, on the Cenotaph in London: 'The glorious dead.' Lieutenant John Kipling's name is inscribed on Burwash's memorial, which was erected in 1920. The memorial also features, rather movingly, a lantern that is lit to mark the anniversary of the death of every villager commemorated.

In 1902, Kipling bought Bateman's, a Jacobean country house on the edge of the village, where he lived until his death in 1936. His wife bequeathed the house to the National Trust and it has been open to the public ever since. The rooms are left as they were when Kipling and his family lived there, including his book-lined study, his inkpot and pen and his pipe.

Brightling and Mad Jack's mausoleum

The landscape around Burwash has hardly changed since Kipling's day, but travel back further to the 1600s, and this quiet valley thronged with the sounds of a vast iron industry that forged the guns and canon of the nation's ships. The Wealden iron industry brought great riches to the Burwash area, particularly the Fuller family who settled in the tiny neighbouring village of Brightling.

Below left: A view of Brightling across the rooftops.

Below right: The Pyramid Folly at Brightling Parish Church.

John Fuller (1757–1834) reaped the rewards of the previous generations' industry, inheriting a fortune in Sussex estates and Jamaican plantations from an uncle when he was only 20. John went on to become an MP, best known for his support of slavery, and for drunken episodes that led to his nickname 'Mad Jack'. The Batsford guide describes him as 'a man of great size. In the House of Commons he was known as the "Hippopotamus". Offered a peerage by Pitt [the Younger], he threw the letter in the fire, remarking, "Jack Fuller I was born and Jack Fuller I will die".'

Jack spent much of his wealth on patronage (he supported the scientist Michael Faraday and bought paintings by J.M.W. Turner) and building unusual structures, which include an observatory in Brightling and the Belle Tout Lighthouse at Beachy Head. When he died, he was buried beneath a 25ft (7.6m) high pyramid in Brightling churchyard, which he built intending it as his final resting place. Legend has it that he is buried inside sitting up in full evening dress with a roast chicken in one hand and a glass of claret in the other. It is certainly a tribute to his larger-than-life character and eccentricities.

Below: The new 'Revolutionary' cricket bat in production at the Gray-Nicholls factory, Robertsbridge in 1975.

Robertsbridge, home of the cricket bat

Every summer, English village greens come alive with the familiar sights and sounds of the cricket match. One Sussex village in particular has a close connection with the game: Robertsbridge is the home of the English cricket bat. In 1856, a local carpenter called Levi J. Nicholls made a bat for his brother and 160 years later, bats are still being made in the village. The business has moved from its original premises and, in the 1940s when the company merged with another bat manufacturer Grays, changed its name to Gray-Nicholls, but the bats are legendary. Here's what W.G. Grace had to say about his on 6 October 1895: 'Dear Sir, I used one of your bats at Hastings in 1894 and I scored one hundred and thirty one. I used it when I made my hundredth century and scored a thousand runs in May with it. So, I think I may call it my record bat.'

Gray-Nicholls is now a global business selling 60,000 bats a year. Although the company has factories in Australia and India, all the bats are made from English willow that has passed through Robertsbridge. The majority are produced overseas but top players still come to the village to have theirs specially crafted to their particular requirements.

Hopping and puffing in Bodiam

Travel through Sussex and Kent and the chances are that at some point you will spot an oast house or two. Many of these buildings, with their distinctive conical roofs topped by a spinning cowl, have been converted into much-admired houses, but their original purpose was to dry hops. 'Oast' is the Kentish word for kiln, and the hops were spread out on perforated floors and dried by air rising from a furnace below.

Hops were an important crop until just a few decades ago and nowhere more so than outside the walls of Bodiam Castle. Surrounded by 850 acres (344ha) of hops, it was the largest area of hops in the country. Every year, during the first two weeks of September, pickers travelled down from London's East End on the train to bring in the crop. At hop-growing peak (in around 1880) 200,000 people, mainly women and children, made the journey to Kent and East Sussex for the hop harvest.

As the hop industry declined, so did the railway and the Kent and East Sussex Railway closed in 1961 – but only for 13 years. Enthusiasts have restored the engines and the line and it has reopened as a heritage steam railway. It now runs a total distance of 11½ miles (18.5km) from Bodiam to Tenterden – the perfect way to survey the fields that once brimmed with hops.

Kent

Biddenden's legend of the maids

Most of Kent, like its neighbour Sussex, was once thickly wooded and sparsely populated. Growing crops and grazing animals was difficult among the trees and scrub, so the early settlers felled trees and cleared the land to create pastures, or 'dens' as they were known. 'Den' is the Old English word for clearing and it forms part of the names of some of the prettiest villages in the county: Tenterden, Smarden, Rolvenden, Bethersden, Benenden and Biddenden.

In 1920 the *Daily Mail*, prompted by comments made by Prince Albert, Duke of York, ran a nationwide competition to improve the quality of village signs. As a result, signs placed at the entrance to the village or on the village green became ornamental, often made from iron, and included something that represented the village. One of the winners was Biddenden whose sign featured the Biddenden Maids on top of a gold and white pole.

The story behind the women, whose names are said to be Mary and Eliza Chulkhurst (although this is open to debate), was recounted in the Batsford guide: 'The village has crazy paving, leaving half-timbered cottages, a row of black and white almshouses and above all, an attractive legend on which it thrives. Here lived England's first recorded Siamese twins, the Biddenden Maids. So devoted were they that when one died, the other refused to be severed from her sister.'

Born in 1100, the twins lived for 34 years conjoined at the shoulder and hip. Doctors proposed to separate the dead sister from her living sibling but she refused saying 'as we came together, we will also go together', and died six hours later. Their will bequeathed their land to the local church, and the income raised provided an annual dole to the poor of the village. As the Batsford guide says:

'At Easter time, the poor and needy would receive a loaf of bread, a pound of cheese and a nice packet of tea.'

The tradition continues today with tea, cheese and bread given to local widows and pensioners, together with a Biddenden cake, baked until it is hard and kept as a souvenir.

Above: Biddenden village sign showing conjoined twins Eliza and Mary Chulkhurst.

Above: Upnor Castle on the banks of the River Medway.

Upnor and the Raid on Medway

For centuries, Royal Navy ships sailed majestically from the Royal Dockyard at Chatham past the villages of Lower and Upper Upnor along the River Medway towards the sea. The villages, which sit on the bank of the river (Upnor derives from the Old English for 'at the bank'), have always had a strong maritime connection: until the 20th century the only way you could reach them was by boat.

The villages have also witnessed one of the worst defeats in English naval history: the Raid on the Medway by the Dutch. Upnor Castle, which was built in 1567 for Queen Elizabeth I, was intended to defend the dockyard and the naval ships moored on the Medway. When tested in 1667, however, it proved ineffectual. A Dutch raiding party, knowing that English ships were virtually unmanned and unarmed due to lack of funding following the plague and the

Great Fire of London, made an audacious assault on battleships moored in the river. Although gunfire from Upnor Castle provided some resistance, it was not enough to prevent the Dutch capturing and towing away two ships including the flagship of the English fleet, HMS *Royal Charles*. The raid was disastrous for King Charles II, and precipitated an end to the war with a favourable peace for the Dutch.

The Royal Navy left the Medway in 1984 but boats still sail past the cobbled streets and weatherboard houses of Upnor – only these days it is yachts and pleasure craft rather than Dutch invaders.

Birchington-on-Sea, home of the British bungalow

With the arrival of the railways in the mid-1800s and the introduction of bank holidays in 1871, came the British people's discovery of the seaside holiday. Most Londoners headed straight for the north-east corner of Kent and to Margate, described rather snootily by the Batsford guide: 'there is a surprising lack of sophistication about London's most popular seaside resort'.

Those with more refined aspirations headed along the coast to Birchington-on-Sea and to the Beresford Hotel. This smart destination, which has since been demolished, was perched on the cliffs overlooking the sea and attracted guests including Harold Wilson, John Betjeman, Adam Faith, Petula Clark and the Beatles. Apart from being a hangout for the great and the good, there was something unusual about the building itself: it was a bungalow – albeit a rather smart and extensive one. And it was not the only bungalow in the village; Birchington had a whole estate of bungalows, the first in the country.

Built in 1877, these single-storey homes were aimed at 'gentlemen of position and leisure' and were the brainchild of architect John Pollard Seddon. Seddon wanted to create a seaside destination for the more discerning visitor and based his designs on large houses with sloping roofs and verandas that he had seen in India (bungalow derives from the Indian word 'bungler'). These substantial houses became second homes for Londoners to escape to for summer weekends. Only four of the original bungalows have survived, but other modern versions have sprung up and with them a lively, year-round community, not just weekenders.

Right: A storm shelter at Minnis Bay, Birchington.

DEVON AND CORNWALL

Devon and Cornwall are two counties rich in history and with strong identities forged from their Celtic origins, but the customs and traditions of the south-west peninsula often go unnoticed as we breeze through on our holidays. With a little curiosity however, a world of ancient customs, indomitable individuals and friendly villages opens up, as does a greater understanding of its people and its places.

Devon has two coasts, north and south, each with its own fishing towns, beaches and resorts. It also has Dartmoor, the largest open space in southern England, and Exmoor, a great stretch of wilderness. Villages are hidden in river valleys or swathed in ancient woodland. It is a county where traditions are kept alive, valued and enjoyed.

Devon

Combe Martin's silver rush, Earl of Tyrone hunt

'Combe' is Devonian for valley, a highly appropriate name for this village in the Combe Valley, which has a long, thin outline that stretches for a mile (1.6km) and between the hills to the sea. Nowadays, with its holidaymakers enjoying the beach and busy cafés, it feels like a classic seaside resort. It wasn't always so peaceful however.

In the 13th century silver was discovered in the hills overlooking the village. Mines soon peppered the landscape with lucrative amounts of silver extracted on and off for 600 years until 1880. Local mining enthusiasts uncovered one of the old shafts, Harris's mine, 30 years ago and are working to preserve it. The ore that was mined is called galena, the natural mineral form of lead (II) sulphide, which contains a high percentage of silver (more than anywhere else in the country). During the reign of Edward I in the late 13th century, the mine was especially productive with miners brought from Derbyshire and South Wales to extract the ore. Mining continued for centuries, and in 1702 an assay office opened in Exeter, which stamped local silverware with a distinctive hallmark featuring a three-towered, turreted castle.

None of Combe Martin's villagers became rich from silver mining, however, as laws stretching back to the Norman Conquest made precious metals like silver the property of the Crown. Some silver mined here even made its way into the Crown Jewels, and a large part of the war expenses of Edward III and Henry V were paid for by the sale of silver mined here.

There are few traces of mining history still evident in the village, but there is one ancient tradition that is still very much alive: the Hunting of the Earl of Rone. In the 17th century the Earl of Tyrone was a leading figure in the Irish resistance to English rule. In 1607 he took flight and, so the story goes, became shipwrecked on a nearby beach. The local grenadiers were called in to hunt him down, an activity re-enacted annually by the villagers on Spring Bank Holiday weekend. Once he has been caught by the grenadiers, Hobby Horse, Fool and the villagers, the Earl is mounted back-to-front on a donkey and paraded through the village to the sea. He is shot at by the grenadiers and when he falls he is revived by the Hobby Horse and the Fool and placed back on the donkey. When the procession reaches the beach the Earl is shot for the final time and an

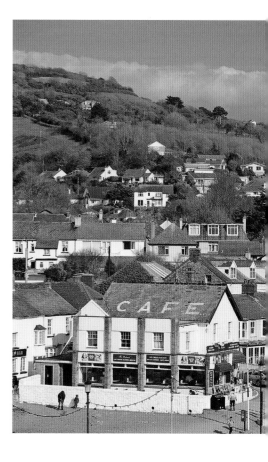

Above: The beachside café at Combe Martin.

effigy is thrown into the sea accompanied by much dancing and drinking.

No one knows how this curious custom started and what is even more puzzling is that the Earl actually found his way safely to Europe. But why let the truth get in the way of a colourful ritual and a jolly good party?

Clovelly, an unlikely place for a village

The 80 homes that make up Clovelly have clung to the cliffs for at least eight centuries. The steep, narrow street that leads down towards the sea is not suitable for cars, so all visitors must park outside the village, and all deliveries are made on a sledge. Unless you live in the village, you must pay to enter, but it is worth the price: the single cobbled street is lined with immaculately presented cottages made from stone and cobb (a mixture of earth, sand and straw typical of the area), and runs for half a mile (0.8km) dropping 400ft (122m) to the sea at a 30-degree gradient. J.M.W. Turner and Charles Dickens were both Clovelly enthusiasts, as was Sir Brian Cook Batsford, the illustrator of the Batsford guides.

The reason for the admission price is that, for three centuries, the village has been privately owned by the Rous family. The current owner is John Rous, whose challenge is to maintain a living village community, manage its upkeep and attract visitors without spoiling its integrity. All Clovelly's residents are tenants and one of the conditions of their tenancy is that they live in their cottages all year. Potential Clovellians are interviewed to make sure they will fit in – and know what they are letting themselves in for. Deliveries are a particular challenge, for example, with neighbours pitching in to help each other haul shopping down from the car park. It is a close community but one that respects the privacy of others – essential if you live in such a confined, though lovely, spot.

Clovelly was built in this unlikely place because it has one of the most sheltered bays on the North Devon coast that, for centuries, provided the ideal spawning ground for huge shoals of herring. During autumn and winter, up to 100 wooden boats known as picarooners would bring in up to 9,000 silver darlings – as the herring were called – on each fishing trip. Loss of spawning grounds destroyed by trawlers, combined with herring quotas and diminishing numbers of fish, has meant that Clovelly is no longer a herring village.

Above (top): A view of Clovelly with the sea beyond.

Above (bottom): Herrings being smoked during the annual Herring Festival in Clovelly.

Cornwall

Cornwall boasts more coastline then any county in the country. The Batsford guide says of the region: 'Towering headlands, rushing streams, precipitous cliffs, woods rising from the water's edge. It is one of the finest stretches of coast scenery in England.'

The coastline was reflected in the evocative illustrations of the guides, which also captured scenes of traditional village life, such as fishermen and their boats and market day in the square. Although the county has changed since the guides were published – there are far fewer fishing boats sailing and the number of markets has dwindled – the coastline remains as dramatic and thrilling as it ever was.

Porthcurno, telegraphs and a teetering theatre

Tucked around the headland from Land's End is a remote village that became an unlikely hub of the British Empire. From 1870 onwards, Porthcurno was the terminus of submarine telephone cables. Using Morse code, the cables allowed Britain to communicate with the world. Telegraphs took nine minutes to reach India from Britain, travelling from Porthcurno to Carcavelos in Portugal, from Carcavelos to Gibraltar, from Gibraltar to Malta, from Malta to Alexandria, and finally, from Alexandria to Bombay. At each stop, the simple Morse message was picked up, retyped and sent onwards. It seems slow and laborious now in the age of direct-dial telephones and broadband, but it was a huge step forward for telecommunications at the time. This tiny village was the largest telegraph station in world and at the forefront of global technology. And it all happened from a simple wooden hut on a Cornish cliff.

By the 1900s, a substantial community had grown up around the telegraph station, and proved resourceful at providing its own entertainment. In 1929, an outdoor performance of *A Midsummer Night's Dream* proved a great success and led to the creation of Porthcurno's other claim to fame, the Minack Theatre.

During the 1920s, Rowena Cade, owner of the Minack headland, had provided space for outdoor productions on her land. As they grew in popularity and scale, she began to make costumes and then, against all the odds, decided to build a theatre on the rocky cliff edge with her own hands. Aged 38, she fetched sand, carried beams, poured cement, carved the auditorium

Left: The clear, green waters of the sea at Porthcurno.

CORNISH VILLAGE NAMES

There is a 17th-century rhyming couplet: 'By tre, pol and pen. Ye shall know all Cornish men.' Those prefaces are all words from the Cornish language and their translation is a helpful way of understanding the topography of the county.

Cos: forest or wood, e.g. Coswarth
Hayle: estuary, e.g. the town of Hayle
Pen: headland, e.g. Penzance
Perran: St Piran, the patron saint of Cornwall, e.g. Perranporth

Pol: pool, e.g. Polruan
Port: port or harbour, e.g. Portreath
Porth: cove, e.g. Porthcurno
Tre: a homestead and its nearby buildings, a settlement, e.g. Tregothnan
Treth: beach, e.g. Portreath
Towan: sand dunes, e.g. Gwithian Towans
Wheal: a mine, e.g. Wheal Jane

out of granite and built the seating into the rock. The result is a thrilling and spectacular outdoor theatre with the turbulent Atlantic Ocean as a backdrop. Every performance at the Minack is literally a cliffhanger.

The first production, *The Tempest*, took place in 1932 – an entirely appropriate play for the wild setting. Rowena continued working on the theatre for 50 years – some of the sets she made when she was 79 are still in use. The theatre has grown and developed over the years, along with its reputation. There is a full programme of productions from April to September every year, with each one embracing the challenges of the unique al fresco stage. The 250,000 visitors who come every year are testament to one woman's vision, hard work and determination.

Tregothnan's tea plantation

The Boscawen family has lived on the Tregothnan Estate near Truro for nearly 700 years, during which time they have created Cornwall's largest private botanical garden. The 100 acres (40.5ha) benefit from the mild air of the Gulf Stream, which produces ideal growing conditions for camellias and rhododendrons, among other shrubs and trees, and from its location – tucked away in a sheltered creek.

One of the more surprising plants to have been introduced to Tregothnan, and which has grown into a successful business, is tea. Tea was first imported to the UK in the 1600s, and was taken up with alacrity by the British people: we now drink 165 million cups a day. The original Tregothnan tea plants came from Darjeeling in 1999 and the plantation now covers 80 acres (32.4ha). Conditions in Cornwall, in terms of rainfall, temperature and soil pH are surprisingly similar to Darjeeling. The tea plant is of the same genus as the camellia, which Tregothnan pioneered in Britain 200 years ago, so was a perfect fit. Now we can all enjoy that most British of drinks, a cup of tea, knowing that is was actually produced here too.

Above: The camellia maze at Tregothnan.

Busveal and the cradle of Methodism

Copper and tin mining dominated Cornish life until the early 20th century, providing employment for many and shaping the landscape, the towns and the villages. Mining was a perilous, poorly paid and exhausting occupation, and as it expanded during the mid-18th century, many miners embraced a new emerging branch of Christianity that offered them hope and a code for living: Methodism.

The tiny hamlet of Busveal played a significant role in the growth of this new faith because it had a ready-made amphitheatre – a hollow called Gwennap Pit – which was formed when mining activities caused the land to sink. It was the perfect place for John Wesley, the founder of Methodism, to preach as it had remarkable acoustics and up to 20,000 miners and their families at a time came from all over Cornwall to listen to his message. Wesley was an inspirational speaker – his fresh and enthusiastic message contrasted with the then-remote and middle-class Church of England. He spoke at Gwennap Pit 18 times between 1762 and 1789, and it was here that he witnessed what he described as 'the most magnificent spectacle which is to be seen this side of heaven. And no music is to be heard upon earth comparable to the sound of many thousand voices when they are all harmoniously joined together, singing praises to God and the Lamb.'

After Wesley's death, the local community constructed the 12 tiers of seating that are still used today for Methodist rallies, as well as plays, musical events and even weddings.

Polruan and troy boats

The Fowey Estuary is one of Cornwall's great natural harbours. Its deep waters have seen everything from tin to pilchards shipped out and, most likely, a fair amount of contraband shipped in. For 500 years, there has also been a ferry service that sails from Fowey to the village of Polruan, taking children to school and ferrying locals and visitors across the estuary. These days the ferry is operated by Alan Toms, a boatman through and through, and an enthusiast for another quite different local sailing craft: the troy boat.

Unique to the Fowey Estuary, and designed for racing, troy boats have been built and sailed competitively from the Royal Fowey Yacht Club since 1929. Only 28 have ever been built (six in the last six years), so ownership of a boat

Above: John Wesley, the founder of Methodism.
Left: Gwennap Pit, the natural amphitheatre at Busveal.

is a rare and valued thing. (The name, by the way, comes from Troy Town, the fictional name given to Fowey by local writer Sir Arthur Quiller-Couch.) With a deep hull and a lot of sail, they are the perfect craft for sailing in a breezy estuary like Fowey.

During the summer, troy races take place twice a week, attracting a dedicated and competitive bunch of sailors. Alan Toms dominates the races with frequent wins, although the contest is always fierce. Life here may have changed since the troys first raced in 1929, but it is reassuring that boats are still bringing people together.

Below: Boats on the water at Fowey Estuary.

Below (left to right): Ancient stained glass in St Neot Church; The 'King' with the garland on Oak Apple Day.

St Neot and Oak Apple Day

During the English Civil War (1642–51), the village of St Neot, on the southern edge of Bodmin Moor, was staunchly royalist. So, when the English monarchy was restored in May 1660, the villagers had a good reason to rejoice – and they have been celebrating every year ever since.

Oak Apple Day was once a formal public holiday all over England. Traditional celebrations involved the wearing of oak apples and oak leaves to represent the oak tree that Charles II hid in when he escaped Oliver Cromwell's Roundheads following the Battle of Worcester in 1651. The public holiday intended 'as a day of thanksgiving for our redemption from tyranny and the King's return to his Government', was eventually abolished in 1859, but St Neot paid no attention. Every May, the vicar leads the villagers, many wearing oak leaves, on a procession through the village. The Tower Captain carries an oak bough, the history of the event is retold and then the vicar blesses the branch before the Tower Captain throws the branch from the tower and hauls up a new one. The tradition is also an excuse to get together, dress up in 17th-century costume, then head off to the vicarage for a drink and a knees-up. As a result, it is one tradition with a good chance of continuing for many years to come.

CORNWALL'S FISHING VILLAGES

Fishing has shaped Cornwall's coastal villages. The stone cottages that fill up with holiday-makers every summer were once the homes of fishermen. And although some harbours are still active, with boats leaving daily to bring back a catch, many have become scenic backdrops for visitors' photographs.

When fishing was central to Cornwall's economy it was a different story. A village like Cadgwith on the Lizard Peninsula would see Cornish luggers, with their distinctive pairs of red sails, arriving and departing all year round. Cadgwith has all the characteristics of a typical fishing village: cottages made of cob, houses constructed from local stone built along the beach and up the valley, and a sheltered harbour with boats moored around it.

Like many other villages, Cadgwith depended on pilchards for its prosperity. Up until the 1950s, pilchard fishing was a thriving industry. The fish were plentiful, with large shoals caught in huge 'seine' nets hung from boats, co-ordinated by lookouts known as huers who would alert the fishermen that a shoal was in sight. In 1904, a record 1,798,000 pilchards were landed in four days. Eventually, over-fishing led to its decline and now the main catch is crustaceans like crab and lobster.

INDEX

Picture credits